Your True
VOICE

Your **T**r u e
VOICE

JESSICA BAILEY

Your True Voice by Jessica Bailey

Copyright © Jessica Bailey 2025

Typeset in Sabon and Acumin Pro

A Cataloging-in-Publications entry for this title is available from The National Library of Australia.

ISBN   978-0-6456069-3-5

10 9 8 7 6 5 4 3 2 1

CHAPTERS

Phase 1: The Unveiling. *This is where the masks fall. Where the illusions, old programs, and limiting beliefs are exposed and confronted. A raw, honest, and sacred shedding.*

Phase 2: The Awakening. *This is the moment you hear your soul clearly. A rising from the ashes. You begin to move with intention, connect to your calling, and recognise your power.*

Phase 3: The Becoming. *Here, you embody your truth. You step fully into your identity, own your story, and begin to show up with bold authenticity. Your voice becomes your compass.*

Phase 4: The Rise. *The final phase. Not the end, but a return to self—elevated. You now lead with wisdom, speak with soul, and move in alignment. This is your era of soulful power and visibility.*

INTRODUCTION

I was born in a small Nigerian village. We had mud huts, bush, stars, and the whispers of spirits and ancestors calling from beyond the trees. No electricity. No hum of machines or warm yellow bulbs. When darkness fell, it was complete. The night devoured everything.

We circled fires, our faces flickering as the flames danced. Our elders told stories; not sweet fairy tales, but sacred myths. Of strange lands, flying metal beasts, and White people with minds second only to that of Jesus Christ. They lived high above us, in planes big enough to swallow our whole village that groaned over our rooftops once a month.

The sky belonged to the White man. We belonged below them.

After my father died, my mother carried us all. She was barefoot, unbowed, and had a spine like steel. I vowed to grow up and succeed, to use my future to buy her freedom. So, when a White man twice my age offered me salvation, I said yes.

How does a village girl—born to a lineage that had never crossed African borders—find herself in the belly of the world she was taught to fear, admire, and obey? Crossing the sea didn't wash away the words written into my mind.

At the age of 22, I found myself in Australia. The land of the White man.

The gods of my childhood stories now walked beside me. Those I had imagined living among the clouds now stood beside me in grocery aisles and train stations.

My husband was White. His family were White. I lived in a White man's home, and I knew my place: **slave.** That's the word my elders used. I had made it into the airplane we once gazed at from the red dirt roads, but I was expected to stay on the floor. If they laid out a mat for the dog and pointed me there, I was meant to **thank them.**

Everything about me felt wrong in this new world. From the moment I arrived, the air pressed differently against my skin. My accent was wrong. My skin too dark. My hair—buried beneath synthetic wigs—was a cry for assimilation. The script I'd inherited told me to whisper when I wanted to roar. My voice, my presence, my existence—it all seemed like a disruption. So I shrank. I walked around carrying the invisible weight of shame and inferiority. And loneliness. God, the loneliness.

Grief rose in me. Grief for a dream that wasn't even allowed to be born.

I'd walk the streets and see African women—almost always in healthcare uniforms—pushing wheelchairs as they pushed through exhaustion. It was clear. No one had to tell me where we belonged. My elders were right. The White masters remained at the top. We stayed at the bottom. And it was only safe for us if we didn't question it.

But in all that misery, one thing stayed: storytelling. My oldest friend and first love. Under the lemon tree in my husband's backyard, I'd sit for hours. My tears became ink, and my silence became stories.

Life was soft at that point—comfortable, even. There was food in the fridge. Bills were paid. I could have stayed in that ease, numbed out in survival mode. But something in me, small and steady, whispered **get ready.** One day, this comfort would end. I had a widowed mother and four younger siblings in Nigeria. I knew that my Australian husband wouldn't shoulder my load forever.

So, I did what I was told. I chose the safe path. I enrolled in nursing, like so many other immigrant women. I was told it was a sensible and secure option for a respectable future. But from the very first day, my spirit began to protest. Wearing the uniform felt like being in someone else's skin. Every day was a nightmare I couldn't wake up from. The shoes got heavier, the halls became longer, the air grew staler. I started to hate my life. I didn't want this. I wanted to tell stories. I wanted to write, to create, to **live.**

Would I ever have that freedom?

During nursing practical sessions, I would hide in the toilet, just trying to make the days disappear. That's how desperate I was for time to pass, for something to shift. One day they told us we had to visit the mortuary.

My soul stood up, flipped the table, and shouted, **absolutely not.**

If dealing with dead bodies was part of the nursing journey, then the universe had just handed me an off-ramp. I believe that my fear of corpses was a warning sign from something greater than me. Something knew this moment would come, and they gave me the exit plan.

I quit. And for once, I didn't explain myself. I left nursing with no regrets, and the thrill of freedom was electric. I rolled up my sleeves in front of my husband's laptop, which felt like treasure. For years, I'd poured my soul into tattered 80-page exercise books, each one bursting with ink-stained dreams. But here I was now, touching keys instead of pages, watching my words bloom on a glowing screen. It felt like Christmas morning, every day. I would write from morning until night, uninterrupted. I returned to the stories I had once whispered under mango trees, which I'd buried beneath the weight of survival. I reached out to Nigerian filmmakers and directors, trying to breathe life into something new that felt real to me.

In Australia, goals seemed too vast, too unachievable. The land itself felt like a giant, towering above me. I didn't belong. I didn't speak the right way. I didn't seem to have the intelligence to belong here. I didn't even know how to open a bank account. My husband came with me to doctor's appointments, because I was terrified. The doctors were White. The system was White. I didn't believe I could answer questions about my own body. That's how deep my fears ran.

Then one day, I shared an idea for a film with a stranger I'd just met. It was casual. I wasn't expecting anything. Well, maybe I was. But I was disappointed. Weeks later, he found me again. His name was Chris. 'I couldn't stop thinking about your story,' he said over coffee. 'The way you tell it, it's like watching a movie.'

That hit something buried deep in me. Back in school, when I used to retell movies to my classmates, they'd crowd around, hanging onto every word as I brought scenes to life with nothing but my voice. I thought it was just play. A childhood habit. But now, years later, a stranger said the same thing and suddenly, it seemed that the gift I'd always carried was speaking out loud. 'Why don't you give this a go in Australia?' he said. 'I'll support you.'

And just like that, the door cracked open.

Soon enough, I would understand just how divinely orchestrated his presence in my life was. It was as if the universe had planted him on my path. He barely knew me, yet he looked at my raw, trembling **passions** and saw brilliance. He saw the spark buried under fear and fog and refused to let it dim. Chris's unwavering belief, paired with the quiet support of my husband, became my wings.

I enrolled in a filmmaking degree. A leap so bold that it didn't make sense for someone like me. Filmmaking, at the time, promised me absolutely nothing. No job. No regular income. No defined path. I spent months searching online for African-Australians in film, hoping to find a role model or a roadmap. But the screen just stared back at me. No footsteps to follow. No proof that this path had ever sustained someone like me.

From the very first day of class, I froze. The other students' words glided effortlessly off their tongues. Their laughter came easy. Their long, glossy hair didn't need fixing. They had perfectly moulded faces, stylish clothes that looked effortless, and a presence that seemed to belong. My elders were right, I thought—these people must be second only to Jesus Christ. My heart pounded as I tucked myself quietly into a corner, doing everything I could to disappear. I had made a mistake. I didn't belong here. The ground could open up and swallow me, and I wouldn't fight it. I felt like a newborn, clueless and slow, and the knowledge I carried from Nigeria had no value here.

Time passed, but the contrast only increased. I stayed quiet. Silence felt safer than humiliation. I had no friends. No one saw me as their equal, and I didn't see myself as one either. When it was time to form groups for class projects, everyone paired off with excitement, and I was left behind. I was begging to help, even in the smallest ways. Serve tea. Hold a light. Anything.

No one spoke to me unless it was task-related. During lunch breaks on set, I sat alone while everyone else laughed together like family. I felt like the hired help, only seen when needed. My jokes didn't land. My references meant nothing. We had no common ground.

'I'm quitting,' I told Chris. 'I don't need this. I have food, I have shelter, and I'm not desperate enough to keep walking through this fire.' Every time I said it, the silence got heavier. Then my safety net was ripped away. My husband lost his job. Alcohol became his weapon of choice; I became the target. I was kicked out of the house while pregnant with our second child. In Nigeria, my mother landed in the ER and needed money. And I still had a degree to finish. It felt like I was collapsing under the weight of too many lives—mother, wife, immigrant, student, ghost.

Chris would say to me, 'I've got your back.' He rented a room in a share house for me. He paid my fees. He created a safe space for me to complete my studies. I cried in silence and studied like my life depended on it. I gave birth, then I thought I could finally exhale, until people working in the media industry told me my degree would be as good as toilet paper.

Every hardship made me say, 'I should've just gone back to Nigeria.' It became a kind of anthem. And every time, Chris would respond calmly, 'You'll still go to Nigeria. But first, get your degree.' Returning to Nigeria wasn't just an idea anymore—it became the finish line. I couldn't wait to be done.

When the time came, something unexpected happened. A deep, paralysing fear gripped me. As much as Australia hadn't worked out, it felt safer to stay in the struggle I knew than to leap into the unknown. And the news coming out of Nigeria didn't help; stories of unrest, corruption, insecurity. Nothing about it sounded inviting. The Nollywood dream I had been clinging to, the one that had kept me going through dark days, started to lose its shine. The deeper I looked, the more I realised it looked better on the outside than it did on the inside. No real profit, structure or visionary leadership. Just chaos dressed in glitz.

I turned to Chris again and said, 'I've changed my mind. I don't want to go anymore. I'd rather mop floors here than go back to that mess.' But Chris, steady as ever, bought me a return ticket. He said, 'No. You need to go and satisfy that craving. You've carried it for too long. If you don't go now, you'll always regret it. You'll wonder what could've been. Now is the time.'

So, I went.

In Nigeria, surrounded by a sea of Black faces that mirrored my own, I felt something crack open inside me. For years, I had worn a mask shaped by shame and fitted for survival. But here, in this land that had known me before I knew myself, the mask slipped off. I was no longer an anomaly; I was one of many. Whole. Unapologetic. Free.

For six months, I listened to laughter floating through the air like music. There was no need to dilute my accent, no need to explain or translate my existence. I walked the streets in my Black skin: visible, proud, unbothered. That's when I realised: prison isn't always made of bars or concrete. Sometimes, prison is the act of shrinking yourself until you disappear.

Though I no longer belonged in Nigeria, I was going home to Australia with something sacred, armed with the fullness of who I was.

And then, I created **I'm Not a Nurse**—a Screenwest-funded short film. A bold, blazing declaration that held not only my story, but the silenced stories of so many others—those who were told to shrink, to stay quiet, to play it safe. But **I'm Not a Nurse** was never meant to exist solely as a short film. It was too layered, too heavy with meaning to be confined to fifteen minutes on screen. It couldn't unravel the long history behind these experiences, the intergenerational pain, or the systemic barriers that persisted. I wrote and published **I'm Not a Nurse** as a book, allowing the story to take on a new life beyond film festivals. The book became a way to reach audiences who might never step into a cinema.

I began to read books like **Your Soul's Gift** by Robert Schwartz, and everything shifted.

In it, Schwartz writes that we are born into belief systems that are opposite to the truths we came here to live. I saw the soul's template. I became a certified life coach and found myself on stages, speaking to audiences who resonated with the themes of identity, belonging, and the suffocating expectations placed on women of colour in professional spaces. And while my journey is rooted in the African-Australian experience, my message stretches beyond borders and cultures.

I realised that there was a plot that tied everything together: my *soul template*.

The Inherited Narrative

I was handed a script that said **Whites belong at the top, Blacks belong at the bottom.** That myth was broadcast to every child in my village, but I became a protagonist, destined to flip that story on its head and embody a new narrative for generations to come.

The Wound That Became a Compass

My father's death and my mother's suffering weren't random tragedies. Their pain packed my bags with enough fire to cross borders no one in my family had ever crossed. I risked the unknown the same way I had seen movie heroes do: with love, grief, and purpose.

Seeing What Others Missed

In Australia, I noticed that there were no African faces that looked like mine on the tv and movie screens. Most people ignored that absence; it became my assignment to fill it.

A Sacred Collision of Love and Fear

I was given a **passion** the world didn't believe in, and a fear of death so intense that it eclipsed my loyalty to my family. Life placed my mother's desperate need and my deepest dread at opposite ends of the same path, creating a challenge which prepared me for what was to come.

My Passion as a Clue

I chose to become a storyteller because I saw it as a way to free many other people.

Discomfort Becomes Fuel

My ex-husband's house was only a landing pad. Had his job remained secure and the walls stayed comfortable, I might have sunk into an easy, ordinary life. Instead, our tension inside the home became a catalyst. His cruelty sparked a blaze within me; every blow added fuel.

Chris, my Ally

Chris would steady me, encourage me, and remind me of who I was. He was part of the template which offered me something deeper and more valuable than money: a guide.

Reclaiming an Identity

I thought I was going back to Nigeria to surrender. I didn't know that my heritage was a missing puzzle piece. Back in Africa, I found something far more precious: **myself**. The part of me I had hidden to survive in Australia. Being in Nigeria reminded me of who I was before the world told me who to be.

The Journey Birthed my True Voice

This journey gave me a book, a film, and a voice that is rewriting the narratives I once inherited. It spoke to me, and others who have felt invisible, boxed in, or silenced.

I Now Sit Where I Belong

I was raised to believe that Blackness was to be hidden and silenced. But today, the girl some people tried to keep down became a woman they look up to. I am Black, visible, and powerful.

My Life Has a Template, and so does Yours

When I look back now, I see a perfectly crafted plan. Every pain. Every push. Every delay. Every detour. And as a life coach, I've seen it in others too. We all have a *soul template*. A divine *design*. But most of us are sleeping on it.

This book is here to wake you up.

It's about discovering the message your life has for the world: where it came from, how it was revealed, and who it's meant for. It's about the realisation that our lives, as chaotic as they seem, are that way for a reason.

Every chapter is designed to reconnect you with the deeper narrative of your life, the soul underneath the surface, and the sacred *mission* encoded in your design.

Your voice matters. Your wounds speak. Your desires are not random. They are breadcrumbs leading you back to your divine path. A path only you can walk. And now it is time. Time to awaken. Time to rise.

Time to *remember.*

Here's the truth: **the soul is ancient. The soul is wise.** It carries a divine blueprint with specific assignments, unique strengths, and precise timing. But none of it can be activated unless we *remember* that this deeper part of us even exists.

This book is here to help you.

THE SOUL *REMEMBERS*

"Before you were formed in the womb, I knew you."
—Jeremiah 1:5

Our paths are written in the stars long before we arrive.
Before your first breath,
Before the joy,
Before the striving,
Before the trauma,
There was a knowing. A deep, eternal knowing.

You are chosen, carved out of intention, wrapped in divinity, and sent here with purpose.

Somewhere along the way, that memory dimmed. Family named you. Culture spoke. Life happened. Fear trained you. And so, like many of us, you began to walk blindly, unaware that beneath it all, your soul was trying to wake you up. You began to think life was happening **to** you. **You forgot it was happening through you.**

We suffer when we forget who we are. We stumble when we forget why we came. We become lost when we follow an external map and not the one we are each born with.

What makes it worse is that the world has trained us to suppress what the soul *remembers*.

To doubt what we feel. To silence the call. To exchange our divine voice for survival. And so, generation after generation, we inherit patterns, beliefs, and burdens that have nothing to do with our original design.

The soul carries a mantle for its bloodline.
To break cycles.
To rewrite stories.
To set prisoners free.

It's about returning to what you've always been underneath the noise. To awaken the divine within and recognise the threads of your personal story as sacred clues, shaping you for the *mission* your soul has carried. It's a journey to reclaim your voice, your vision, your divine inheritance.

This is your *true self*: the version of you that existed before the world told you who to be.

THE UNVEILING

This is where the masks fall. Where the illusions, old programs, and limiting beliefs are exposed and confronted. A raw, honest, and sacred shedding.

Chapters

◇ **The Soul's Plan**—*Remember* the sacred agreement your soul made before choosing your body as its home.

◇ **The Rise of the Old Belief**—Explore how your limiting beliefs were set up through experiences, culture, and survival mechanisms.

◇ **The Design of Opposition**—Understand how resistance seems to keep you in familiar cycles, and how it's secretly designed to wake you up.

◇ **The Call to Break Free**—Recognise the moment your soul whispered (or screamed) for change, and the restlessness that stirred your awakening.

◇ **Breaking Out of the Cage**—Step into the moment where you challenge the norm, take a risk, and dare to leave comfort behind.

◇ **The Death of the Old Belief**—Witness the collapse of what once defined you, and embrace the grief and liberation that comes with it.

CHAPTER ONE

THE SOUL'S PLAN

The Soul is a Traveller

It is not bound by time, nor by space. It is not defined by the container of flesh it wears, nor the name the container was given at birth. The soul moves. It expands. It journeys.

- To arrive here, in the land of the living, the soul takes *birth* as its *channel*.
- To reach its *mission*, it takes *pain* as its *portal*.
- To return to the land of the spirit, it takes *death* as its *passage*.

These means are sacred. They are **gateways**: soul-designed passages for evolution.

When the soul arrives on Earth, it has only reached the first station: **the body**. The next transition is not physical; it involves the soul's *mission*. But the soul cannot achieve its *mission* without **being refined**.

And what is the soul's chosen vehicle for this refinement? **Pain.**

Pain breaks the shell.
Pain cracks open the illusion.

Pain invites you into remembrance.
Pain activates the part of you that has been asleep.

Without the breaking, there can be no *becoming*.

Growth Is Not Just Physical

When a child is born, we understand that their body must grow over time, with food and nurturing. We forget that the soul must also grow. It arrives with a dream: its *mission*. And before arriving, it lays out the perfect curriculum that will shape it to fulfill that *mission*.

The soul grows through *experiences*—especially the ones we try to avoid. Abandonment, rejection, loss, betrayal, and struggle are the sacred nutrients of soul growth.

Think of it this way: a child might want to be a doctor. We know they can't become a doctor without education, exams, discipline, and practice. So we plot a path. We curate their curriculum. We give them challenges because we know it prepares them for their dream.

In the same way, each soul has made plans **before** arriving.

It chose the body that would house it.

- It chose the family that would shape it.
- It chose the environment that would stretch it.
- It chose the exact set of circumstances, relationships, and even heartbreaks that would prepare it for purpose.

Souls don't make reckless decisions. Each one makes **choices** that are aligned with its *mission*. It chooses what will serve its highest evolution, even if that means discomfort, separation, or struggle in the beginning.

The soul sees what the ego cannot: **everything is leading you back to yourself.**

The Map of the Soul's Journey

Long before you took your first breath, before your body even formed in the womb, something deep and eternal had already stirred into motion. The soul had a plan.

In order to carry it out, the soul designed that plan with a *mission, a portal, and collaborators.*

- *Mission:* Why the soul came. What it came to express, embody, or awaken.
- *Portal:* What pain it will walk through to be refined and where it would come from.
- *Collaborators:* Who will help shape the journey. The people and events—kind and cruel—that activate the soul's *remembering.*

Each of these holds a piece of your story, designed to help you become who you were always meant to be. We're talking about a *strategy*, woven with clarity and intention. The soul didn't just **land** here; it *chose.* And now, your task in this life is to *remember* that **our paths were written in the stars before we were born.**

Part 1. The Soul's Mission

Before you arrived here, your soul made a declaration. It said, **there's a truth the world has forgotten. I will embody that truth. I will become the living story.**

Each soul carries a story it came to *transform*, a light it came to ignite in the world. And in time, as we journey together, you will *remember* what yours is. You see, a soul doesn't come to repeat what already exists. It comes to interrupt the patterns woven through generations, threaded with silence, shame, fear, and smallness. It comes to rewrite the story.

That rewriting happens through you.

Your soul's *mission* is about what you'll do and what you'll become.

- Maybe your soul came to **pull others out of sham**e by walking out of it yourself, as proof that healing is not only possible, it's inevitable.

- Maybe you came to **bridge the divide** between race, class, gender, history, cultures, or even generations of grief.

- Maybe it came to **embody radical forgiveness**—to show the world what love looks like when it has every reason to hate.

Whatever your *mission* is, you came to walk it in real time. To wear it in your body. To echo it through your choices. To **bleed** and **breathe** it, until others can see what was once invisible.

This is your *true voice*. You are the vessel that voice chose to travel through. You are the message the world didn't know it was waiting for. But to embody this message, your soul knew it would need to be shaped.

And that brings us to the second layer of the plan: *the portal.*

Part 2. The Soul's Portal

Every soul that arrives on Earth comes with a *mission* and chooses a specific *portal* that will shape it, humble it, crack it open, and ultimately awaken that voice. That *portal* is **pain**. *Transformation* rarely comes without it. The soul is here to evolve, and nothing sculpts a soul like **pain**.

But **pain** isn't one-size-fits-all. Every soul chooses its own form of refinement.

Some souls choose **abandonment**. They will be born to parents who leave, or into families emotionally unavailable. They will grow up craving connection and learning how to self-soothe, only to discover that their *mission* is to become the love they never received, and to teach others how to build safe, nourishing homes within themselves.

Some choose **rejection**. From schoolyard bullying to romantic heartbreak, job losses to unreturned calls, these souls will constantly meet the word **no** until they embody unshakeable self-worth, teaching the world that their value was never up for negotiation in the first place.

Others pick **loss**. A child, a partner, or a parent gone too soon. The grief feels unbearable. But hidden in that ache is an invitation to build something new. To bring healing where there was only silence.

And then there are souls who choose to be refined by their **passion**. These are the ones who pour their heart into their calling only to find that this path is also their crucible. They are rejected, silenced, misunderstood. But it is through their **passion** that they are both broken and rebuilt. These are the ones who rise with fire in their voice, who will guide others through it too.

Part 3: The Collaborators

This is where the soul's plan becomes truly breathtaking. Because the soul doesn't just choose its **pain**. It chooses the people who will deliver it. They are **collaborators**—souls who, before this lifetime, made a sacred agreement to play a role in your evolution. And here's the part most of us struggle to accept: they're not always the ones who love you sweetly. In fact, many of them will challenge you. They may hurt, betray, abandon, reject, belittle, or block you. But on another level, they were never against you. They are here for you.

Let's break this down.

1. The Allies

These are the rare few who walk beside you. They don't try to fix you or save you. They **see** you. They whisper truth into your silence. They remind you of who you are when you forget. They celebrate your wins and hold space for your wounds.

They may be a friend, a mentor, a guide, or a stranger who spoke one sentence that changed your entire trajectory. They are the soul's gentle helpers. The light-bearers who carry a lamp while you find your way.

Like Amara. She was born into a home where love felt inconsistent; there some days, gone the next. Her father left when she was three. Her mother, though physically present, was emotionally locked behind her own trauma. Amara grew up with a quiet ache. For years, she believed she was unlovable.

She learned to comfort herself, to become her own anchor. For years, she moved through life with this invisible wound, trying to earn love through perfection and performance. But one day, it hit her: this ache wasn't her punishment, it was her *portal* to her true voice.

Her greatest wound became her soul's greatest wisdom.

Her soul hadn't come to Earth just to suffer from **abandonment**. It came to **reconnect**. To become the safe space she had longed for. Today, Amara is a therapist and speaker who helps others return home to themselves. She teaches people how to stop abandoning themselves in the name of love.

2. The Mirrors

These collaborators may not hurt you, but they confront you. It might be the confident friend whose boldness irritates you—until you realise you have been dimming your own light. Or the partner who refuses to rescue you, forcing you to stand in your own strength. Or the child who wants to be with you but tests every ounce of your patience, teaching you how to love without condition.

They reflect what you have not yet owned in yourself. They are here to **reveal you.**

3. The Wounders

These are the ones who play the role of the villain. The ex who lied. The parent who withheld love. The teacher who humiliated you. The colleague who sabotaged your work. Their actions hurt. Deeply. But from a soul's perspective, these individuals are meant to crack you open in all the places where your power has been asleep.

Let me give you an example from my own life.

I was expected to become a nurse. It was the path my community saw as safe and respectable. But something deep inside always resisted. Even when no one around me believed in it, I did. I knew that storytelling was not just a hobby for me, it was a way to *remember*.

Still, my path wasn't easy. I faced racism, rejection, and the sting of being unseen as an artist, and as a **Black African woman**. I was told to keep my head down.

I chose to lift my voice instead. My soul had chosen **passion** as the *portal* because it would burn away every false idea until only my truth remained.

But to speak that message with power, I needed *collaborators*.

My soul chose a grandfather who believed White people were superior, so that I would learn how to remove those beliefs at the roots. It chose institutions that dismissed me, and systems that tried to contain me, so that I could show them my growth and tell a bigger story. It chose lovers who bruised me with silence and violence so I could learn the difference between settling and sacredness. It even chose a mentor who, at my breaking point, reminded me of my own *true voice* when I had forgotten it. Every one of them played their part, helping to birth the woman I had to become.

When you step back, you can see how the betrayals, the heartbreaks, the rejections, and even the silences all fit into a larger choreography.

So, ask yourself:

- Who stood beside you when it was too dark to walk alone?
- Who mirrored your potential before you could see it?
- Who hurt you and awakened you?

These are your *collaborators*, here to activate your *mission*.

They didn't betray the *soul's plan*. They fulfilled it.

◇◇◇◇◇

Chapter Summary

Your soul did not come here by accident—it came with a plan. Before you were born, your soul chose a *mission* to fulfill. It also chose a specific **pain** for *transformation*, and *collaborators*—both kind and cruel—to raise your *true voice*. Pain was never meant to punish you; it was always part of the soul's sacred strategy to awaken your *true voice* and align you with your divine purpose. The task now is simple, yet profound: to *remember*.

◇◇◇

Soul Reflection Questions

1. What moments of pain in my life have shaped me the most, and what strength did they awaken in me?

2. What pattern or pain keeps repeating in my life—and could it be the *portal* to my purpose?

3. If my soul chose this life with intention, what might have been the *mission* I agreed to before birth?

4. Who in my life has challenged me deeply, and what did their presence activate in me?

5. What qualities or truths do I feel I've come to embody or express in the world?

6. Which relationships feel like soul allies—those who see and support my *becoming*?

7. Where in my life am I still waiting for outside validation instead of trusting my inner knowing?

8. How might I reframe my biggest heartbreak or disappointment as a *divine collaboration* for my growth?

9. Have I been rejecting my story, or can I begin to see it as sacred preparation?

10. What am I ready to *remember* about who I am and why I'm here?

CHAPTER TWO

THE RISE OF THE OLD BELIEF

Now, let's understand how souls land on Earth; the mystery of birth.

A child is born and a soul has arrived. The soul is ancient. Timeless. Infinite. This soul has entered a body, a vessel, a form. And while the body is tiny and new, it begins its *mission*, one it chose long before this moment.

From the moment the child is here, the soul starts to take in everything around it. It inhales its environment. It absorbs its parents' unspoken fears, their silent hopes. It takes in the culture, the traditions, the rules of belonging and survival. As a child, the soul is pliable. It yields to its surroundings, not yet able to resist. And so, the world begins to form a story around it; a story that often contradicts its *true voice*:

- You are too much.
- You must stay quiet.
- People like you can't do things like that.

And so, slowly, a false self is built. One that fits the world, but silences the soul. It believes:

- This is who I must be to be loved.
- This is what I must suppress to stay safe.
- This is how small I must become to fit in.

Before it can form its own thoughts, it inherits beliefs:

- If I'm good, I'll be loved.
- If I succeed, I'll be safe.
- If I cry, I'll be weak.
- If I speak up, I'll be punished.
- If I don't fit in, I'll be rejected.

These beliefs are stitched into your sense of self before you have a chance to question them. And while they may protect you, they also cage you. They shaped your worth in terms of obedience, performance, and approval. Invisible, yet limiting, this cage began to shape the soul's early identity. The soul, once so clear and radiant in its knowing, now begins to forget. Not because it is weak, but because forgetting is part of the journey to *remembering.*

This is where the inner tension begins. Because deep within, the soul *remembers* what the mind does not. There is a divine unrest. A sacred discomfort. A holy ache that no success or performance can silence. The soul arrives whole, carrying its *true voice* within but lands in a world where everything is opposite to that truth. A world built to contradict the soul.

Before it can be made, it must be broken. This is preparation. *True voice* is forged in the fire of contradiction. It must walk through everything that would try to silence it.

The soul must experience what it is not, in order to remember **what it truly is.**

So, the soul descends into an illusion built from inherited beliefs and absorbed without question. The soul builds its identity around what it has learned, not what it *remembers*. It does not yet know why certain patterns repeat, why **pain** follows like a shadow, why it longs for something it cannot name.

This is the *Ordinary World*; the beginning of the soul's sacred story.

Life in the Ordinary World

This world appears normal. School. Family. Friends. Work. You tick the boxes. Say the right things. Here, you live unaware, quietly aching, unknowingly preparing. Life is predictable. Repetitive. A rhythm without resonance. But underneath it all, something stirs. It feels like you're watching your life through a window, unable to go play outside. You're praised for fitting in, but you quietly wonder if you've betrayed something sacred inside you.

You smile in photos. You fulfill your obligations and expectations. You follow the rules. But something inside still feels hungry. Not for food, not for success, but for something deeper. Something true. You don't have the language for it, you just know **this isn't it.**

There is no great enemy here. No dragons to slay, only a subtle disconnection. The hero does not yet know that there is a quest to undertake. But the ache is real. This is the setup. The sleep before the stirring.

The Invitation Is Coming

Even in the midst of the illusion, your purpose is not gone—it's just sleeping. It's there, buried beneath perfectionism, people-pleasing, and the pressure to be enough.

Sometimes it stirs when the world goes quiet, in moments of deep discomfort. Sometimes it appears through your resistance, your art, or your restlessness. This tension you feel is a holy dissatisfaction, planted to call you home.

One day—through loss, heartbreak, rejection, wonder, or a mysterious moment of clarity—you will be invited to leave the

Ordinary World behind. You will be called into the very journey your soul came to walk.

My invitation came with *an inherited belief.* **Whites belong at the top, Blacks belong at the bottom.**

Power belonged to the White man, as my grandparents would say. They built the cities. They wrote the future. When one of their airplanes flew over our village once a month, we'd run barefoot to watch it split the sky. They lived above. We stayed below. That was the order.

I come from a line of survivors who didn't have time for their **passions**—they had work to do. They sacrificed. They endured. Dreams weren't on the menu; survival was. I inherited other deep-rooted beliefs, too. **Passion is dangerous. Dreams lead to disappointment. Practicality is power.**

But I didn't just arrive on this planet with skin and breath. I came carrying an ancestral love for storytelling that pulsed in me before I even had words. Stories lit me up. Images danced in my mind. I could create whole worlds inside me. But in my world, storytelling was not a path. It was a pastime. A luxury. A dream for people with the right skin, the right passport, the right place in the story. And so, like my ancestors before me, I traded stories for survival. I buried the fire. I took the safe road.

By the time I arrived in Australia, my inherited belief training was complete. I knew my place. And so, there I was, a young African woman with fire in her bones, standing in a country where that fire is too much. Too loud. Too ambitious. Too Black.

I was like an ant in a boxing ring with a giant.

This is the *portal* of **pain** my soul chose. My love for storytelling was a *mission*, planted before my birth. And when the world said **no**, something ancient rose from within, as if to say **watch me.**

To live my purpose, I had to defy my inheritance. I had to walk through the very system designed to silence me. Break the script. Rewrite the rules. This is where my *transformation* began. The resistance I faced wasn't a wall. It was a mirror.

The elders who told me I'd never have power? They were the very ones who trained me for this fight. They handed me the script so I could rewrite it.

Years later, I stood in front of them with a voice that refused to sleep and a story that refused to serve them. I came to speak for the ones who never got to do it for themselves. I came to write for the ones who were never written in. I came to stand in the fire and to burn brightly.

The Power of Limiting Beliefs

Long before we have language to question them, limiting beliefs have already taken root in each of us. We don't even realise they exist. They whisper, building a cage from the stories we've been told, and the stories we've told ourselves. The door may be wide open, but if your mind believes it's locked, you'll never walk through.

For me, that cage showed up in filmmaking. No one stood in my way. There were no guards at the gate, no one telling me I couldn't create, but I was still waiting to feel **allowed**.

Think about the moments in your life when you wanted to take a leap, dream bigger, or step outside of what was expected, but something held you back.

- You hesitated.
- You second-guessed yourself.
- You convinced yourself it wasn't possible.

That voice wasn't yours. That was an old belief system. They shape your choices, influence your actions, and dictate your life without you even realising it.

- If you believe success is only for a certain kind of person, you won't even try.

- If you doubt your talent, intelligence, or worth, you won't step into spaces where you truly belong.

- If you were raised to think misery is part of life, you won't break the cycle.

Inherited scripts shape how we see the world. They are passed down like family heirlooms, woven into traditions, expectations, and unspoken rules. We absorb them from our parents, our culture, and society at large. These beliefs shape destinies.

So many of us walk away from our dreams because the world tells us they're not realistic. We hear things like:

- 'There's no money in that.'
- 'No one makes it in that field.'
- 'That's not what people like us do.'
- 'Be practical.'
- 'Stick to the plan.'

So we listen. We shrink. We trade what lights us up for what feels safe. We stay in jobs we hate. We chase approval instead of purpose. We settle, because that's what we've been taught. But there's a hidden cost. When we walk away from our *true voice*, we lose a piece of ourselves. We disconnect from the path we were born to walk.

Here's the truth: when you choose the path others expect, you still struggle. This struggle feels like being stuck. Like waking up tired. Like something's missing and you don't know what. Like you're wearing someone else's clothes, living someone else's life. But this is the struggle which brings you back to yourself. It changes you, fuels you, and leads you to make an impact. Because deep down, you know you were meant for more. You feel it in your bones. You hear it in the silence. You carry it in the parts of you you've tried to bury. And that path doesn't stop *calling*.

When you choose your soul's *mission*—the one path that feels true, even if it scares you—you will struggle, and doubt, and fear. But you don't have to run. You can stop and listen.

Because the life that's meant for you is *waiting*.

The Struggle Is the Curriculum

No one starts as a master. We all begin as students. Then we are shaped by struggle, tested by trials, refined by fire. The challenges we face are not roadblocks. They are the tools that carve us into who we are meant to be.

This contrast between who we are and who the world tells us to be is by design.

- It is by design that a person meant to teach abundance is born into lack.
- It is by design that a person meant to heal is deeply wounded first.
- It is by design that a person meant to lead is overlooked, underestimated, or doubted.

Why is this so? Because opposition is necessary. Because without conflict, there is no story. Every hero is placed in a world that challenges them.

I know a soul who arrived on earth with tenderness woven into her bones. She was a natural giver. Sensitive, intuitive, attuned to others before they even spoke. Love was her native language, but very early on, she learned that love came with rules. It wasn't freely given; it had to be earned. And so, her soul adapted.

Her invitation came with an inherited belief: **If I am not needed, I will be left.**

She began to shape herself around the needs of others. If being loud caused disapproval, she became quiet. If being emotional led to others withdrawing, she became unemotional. If asking for something made people leave, she stopped asking altogether. Slowly, she disappeared into the performance of being **enough**. At home, she was the helper. At school, the achiever. In relationships, the caretaker. Always useful, always giving, but never truly seen. She thought her value lived in her ability to hold everyone else together. And she feared that if she ever stopped holding everyone together, they would all walk away.

She was abandoned anyway. A parent who left. A friend who turned cold. A lover who ghosted. A job that discarded her once she stopped over-performing. No matter how much she gave, it was never enough to guarantee permanence. The very thing she feared kept repeating. Not because she was cursed—but because this was her soul's chosen *portal*. Her inherited belief became a cage. It told her to abandon herself first, so others wouldn't do it later.

She didn't know that the soul's *mission* is to undo inherited beliefs. That her true power is in letting herself be held. That her presence will one day heal others simply because she learned to stay true to herself first.

The journey always begins in the opposite of what we are meant to become. Because *transformation* requires training. You cannot teach what you haven't lived. But here's the thing: training only works if you show up for it. So, the question is: **are you willing to accept your chosen journey?**

◇◇◇◇◇

Chapter Summary

Every soul is born into a world of inherited beliefs that shape, shrink, and silence it. These beliefs—unspoken, absorbed, and deeply ingrained—become the soul's first language and begin the performance of survival. But beneath the surface of conformity lies a sacred ache: a longing to *remember*. The soul forgets because forgetting is part of the design, setting the stage for *transformation*. The struggle, the silence, and the inherited beliefs are preparation. Every false identity formed is the setup for the soul's awakening. And though the soul sleeps now, the invitation to rise is waiting.

◇◇◇

Soul Reflection Questions

1. What beliefs about yourself did you absorb before you had words?

2. What parts of yourself did you shrink, suppress, or hide to feel safe or loved growing up?

3. Whose voices shaped your sense of worth, and do those voices still live inside you?

4. What were you praised for as a child, and what did you quietly ache for instead?

5. Where in your life are you still performing to be accepted rather than showing up as your full self?

6. What sacred longing lives beneath your success, your people-pleasing, or your perfectionism?

7. Can you trace any patterns in your life—repeating pain, roles, or fears—that may be linked to an inherited belief?

8. What message or *mission* might your soul have chosen that your circumstances were meant to prepare you for?

9. In what ways is your current discomfort an invitation to **remember**?

10. Whose story are you living—and is it time to write your own?

CHAPTER THREE

THE CALL TO BREAK FREE

There comes a time when the soul can no longer pretend.

This moment builds in silence for months or years. But eventually, the soul reaches its limit of surviving and tolerating. And when it does, it will make itself known. Loud. Raw. Undeniable. Something will break. Something must.

You feel it long before you name it. That slow-burning ache beneath the routine. That restlessness under the surface of your daily life. You wake up tired, not just in your body, but in your spirit. You go to work, perform your duties, say all the right things as something inside you whispers **this isn't it. This isn't who I came here to be.**

Sometimes, the soul will nudge you gently. A dream you can't shake. A vision that keeps returning. A voice inside whispering **more, more, more.**

Sometimes the soul must break you open to set you free. You'll get fired. You'll walk away from the degree. The relationship you built your life around will suddenly end. You'll lose the thing you thought you couldn't live without. Not because life is cruel, but because your soul is trying to save you from a smaller life. For a long time, your soul has tried to keep the peace. It tried to make the life you inherited feel like your own. It wore the mask, played the part. It nodded along to expectations, even when they suffocated its truth. For me, it said yes to nursing school when what it really wanted was to tell stories that awaken the world. It stayed in relationships that felt safe, even though it was dying for freedom. It clocked in at a café, delivering smiles and small talk, while a deeper purpose pulsed quietly with every coffee that was poured.

I know this rebellion well.

After surrendering to nursing in Australia, I convinced myself it was the smart choice. It made sense; it was a stable, respected, safe path that promised hope for my family. But from day one, everything inside me said **no**.

I hated the shoes.
The uniform.
The smell of the labs.
The language: syringe, antiseptic, injection.
It all felt like nails on a chalkboard.

My heart wasn't in the room. It was somewhere else entirely. Somewhere with stories. With the voices of souls speaking their truth. I didn't want to heal bodies, I wanted to **move people**. Every time a nursing tutor opened their mouth, I wanted to turn their words into a stick and beat them into silence. That's how deeply out of place I felt. Dramatic? Maybe.

But it was real. I was unhappy. I was suffocating. I was **boiling**.

The truth is that when your soul isn't in the room, it doesn't matter how good the pay is, how proud your parents are, or how successful it looks from the outside.

You'll always feel like something is missing.

What It Looks Like When Your Soul is Off Track

A lost soul isn't dramatic or obvious.
It often looks like someone **doing everything right but feeling all wrong.**

It looks like:

- A lawyer who really wanted to be a hairstylist.
- A cleaner whose heart beats for journalism.
- An office worker who dreams of creating music.
- A full-time parent who secretly wants to write a book.

Not because those jobs are bad, but because they were never **the way to those souls'** *missions.*

Somewhere along the way, you got the message:

- That dream won't pay the bills.
- That's not what our family does.
- Be realistic, you can't make a living doing that.

And, like so many others, you put on the mask. You followed the script and took the safe road, even though it didn't feel like it would take you home.

The soul does not care about appearances. It doesn't care how long you've invested in a job, a relationship, or a reputation. It came for truth. It came for growth. It came for purpose. And when the time comes, it will do whatever it must to break through.

This is the threshold before *transformation.* You are standing at the edge of everything you've ever known, and it is terrifying, but also sacred. You are not breaking down, you are breaking open. The fire you feel? That's the soul burning off everything that was never truly yours. This is necessary. You came to shed the old skin, to unmask, to rise in the fullness of your *true voice.*

This is the soul's fight to cast off the inherited beliefs and reclaim its throne. This is the soul rising to say **I am here now. I will not be silenced.**

The soul is hungry to show itself. Hungry to lead. Hungry to *remember.*

Jesus knew His moment. He knew when the time had come. And He didn't run. He walked toward the cross because He knew resurrection would only come through breaking. The same is true for you.

So if you feel like something is dying—let it.
If your world feels like it's falling apart—let it.
If everything you thought you were is crumbling—let it.
Your soul is reclaiming you.
Your time has come.
Let the breaking begin.

What Soul Rebellion Looks Like

Imagine a fish flopping on dry land. It doesn't belong there. It can't breathe. And no matter how long it's stuck, it keeps trying to get back to water, because it **knows** it wasn't made for land.

That's exactly what happens when you live a life that doesn't fit you. Your soul knows. And it won't stop fighting until it finds its way home. If you're feeling this discomfort, you're not alone. Here are the signs that your soul is calling you to something greater:

- **You wake up feeling unfulfilled.** Even when there's nothing obviously wrong, things still don't feel right.

- **You don't look forward to work.** Monday mornings feel like a slow death, and you find yourself counting down to the weekend, to retirement, to **something else.**

- **Your creativity feels blocked.** You struggle to come up with new ideas or feel excited about possibilities.

- **You feel trapped.** The idea of spending the next five, ten, or twenty years like this feels unbearable.
- **You feel lost or confused.** You don't know what you want, but you **know** this isn't it.

These are not signs of failure. These are signs that *you are being called to* **break free.**

Souls get tired of tolerating. Tired of postponing a *calling*. Tired of settling for survival and tired of shrinking so that others feel comfortable. Tired of carrying the weight of ancestral beliefs that choose duty over desire; silence over voice; obedience over truth. Something is stirring, and it will not be silenced. This is the soul preparing to rise.

There was a time I walked through life like a ghost.
Not dead—just not **here.**
Everyone else seemed to know what to do.
They got up. Got dressed. Went to work.
Laughed at lunch. Made weekend plans.
Lived lives that looked like they fit.

Me? I floated on the edges. Nothing fit.
Not the jobs. Not the conversations. Not the rhythm.

At the end of each year, when the world paused to celebrate or plan,
I slipped into the quiet places, like a park bench under a jacaranda tree.
Shoes off, head tilted to the sky.
Wondering why I couldn't just be **normal.**
Why the act of dreaming felt too big.

Sadness didn't knock. It moved in.
Loneliness tucked itself beside me.
And yet, beneath the ache, there was always a flicker.

I didn't know what my soul wanted.
Not exactly.

Only that it felt like **story.** Like **play.**
Like something people might call unserious, but to me
It felt like breath.

And some days, I'd sit in the grass, daydreaming
Not about fame or certainty,
But about what it might feel like
To finally choose **me.**

The Call to Action: The Choice You Must Make

Most people don't break free because they're comfortable. People ignore the call out of fear.

- Fear of the unknown. **What if I step into something new and fail?**
- Fear of judgment. **What will people think if I change?**
- Fear of leaving the familiar. **Even if I'm unhappy, at least I know what to expect.**

Even when we feel stuck and we know things aren't working, there's security in the familiar. The old belief system may be limiting, but at least it's predictable.

- You know how to navigate it.
- You know what to expect.
- You know how to avoid failure.

But deep down, you also know it's holding you back.

Every hero in every great story faces a pivotal moment: *the calling.*

This is the moment when they realise they can no longer continue as they are. They must either:

1. *Stay the same.* Remain in the *Ordinary World*, following the same patterns, trapped in the same **pain** as the generations before.

2. *Step into the unknown.* Break free, challenge everything they've been told, and claim the life their soul was meant for.

And right now, the choice is in front of you.

What Happens If You Answer the Call?

If you answer the call, *you are declaring war.* Not on the world, not on your family, not even on the people who doubt you. You are declaring war on the **old version of yourself.** The one who was willing to settle. The one who kept quiet to keep the peace. The one who put everyone else's expectations before their own. And when you step into this battle, don't expect a warm welcome.

Your first battle might begin with family.

◆ **Are you crazy? What do you think you're doing?**
◆ **You had a good path. Why would you throw it away?**
◆ **What if you fail? What if this doesn't work?**

Your friends might fight with you too.

◆ **Wrong choice.**
◆ **That's unrealistic.**
◆ **Who do you think you are?**

Some will stop calling. Some will distance themselves. Some will roll their eyes when you speak about your vision.

Even your closest relationships might feel the weight of your decision.

Because when you grow, when you step into your soul's *calling,* you **change.** And when you change, the dynamics of your relationships change too. Some partners will support you. Others will feel threatened.

You will have to fight against *your own fear*. The self-doubt will hit harder than any words from others. **You'll have to** fight to stay true to yourself when things around you and within you try to pull you back.

Here's what I want you to know: **you have what it takes.**

You may not feel strong or ready enough now, but if you hold on, trust yourself, and keep walking even when the road feels impossible, you will see what you are made of. That is the whole point of this fight. It's not just about stepping into a new life. It's about proving to yourself who you really are.

You were not born to live a life that suffocates you.
You were not meant to shrink, to conform, to survive on autopilot.

You were meant to **grow**.
To **expand**.
To become **fully alive.**

How to Answer the Call

If you're feeling the call to break free, here's what you need to do:

- Acknowledge it. Stop pushing it down. Recognise that this feeling is real.
- Get curious. Start exploring. Read, learn, talk to people who inspire you. Open yourself to new perspectives.
- Take one small step. You don't have to overhaul your life overnight. Just start moving in the direction that excites you.
- Trust the process. The how doesn't have to be clear yet. Just start.

◇◇◇◇◇

Chapter Summary

The *calling* to break free is a sacred reckoning. It arrives when the soul can no longer tolerate the cage of conformity and demands truth over tradition, purpose over performance. Whether through a whisper or a wake-up call, the soul breaks us open. It doesn't ask for permission; it demands liberation. This is the beginning of *becoming* who you truly are. If everything is crumbling, let it. The breaking brings your freedom.

◇◇◇

Soul Reflection Questions

Use these questions as sacred mirrors to help you discern the places in your own life where your soul is whispering (or shouting) for freedom:

1. What relationships, jobs, or routines feel like cages instead of catalysts?

2. What part of my daily life feels lifeless, draining, or misaligned with who I really am?

3. Where in my life do I feel like I'm doing things to keep the peace or meet others' expectations?

4. What dream or desire keeps returning to me, even if I've tried to silence it?

5. What are the ancestral or cultural beliefs I've inherited that tell me I can't or shouldn't pursue what I want?

6. What fear is currently holding me back from choosing myself and answering the call to break free?

7. What might become possible in my life if I finally gave myself permission to choose me?

8. When was the last time I truly felt alive, and what was I doing, saying, or being in that moment?

9. What would it mean to trust the discomfort in my life as a divine signal—not a problem to fix, but a doorway to truth?

10. If I fully honored my soul today, what one bold step would I take toward freedom?

CHAPTER FOUR

THE BREAKING OUT
OF THE CAGE

If you've made it this far, congratulations. That's no small thing. It takes courage.

Your old beliefs—the one that kept you in place and dictated your every move—aren't just going to disappear because you decided to walk away. They will test you. They will scream at you. They will make you question everything.

And the world will not make this easy for you. Be ready for:

- The voices that say **you're making a mistake.**
- The doubts that whisper **you're not good enough.**
- The guilt that tells you **you're being selfish.**

Be ready to bleed. Because this is where it gets real.

The Moment Everything Changes

For me, this journey started the day I decided to quit nursing studies to pursue filmmaking.

It didn't make sense on paper.
I had responsibilities.
I had a family to support.
I had every reason to keep doing what I had been doing.
But my soul was **suffocating.**

I recall thinking: **F-ck the rules. F-ck the expectations. F-ck living a life that isn't mine.**

I was done pretending.
I was done lying to myself.
I was done playing small.

I left behind a path that guaranteed security. I stepped into a world where nothing was promised, except the feeling that, finally, I was alive.

Was it terrifying? **Absolutely.**
Did I doubt myself? **Every single day.**
Did I know what I was doing? **Not at all.**

But I knew I couldn't stay where I was.

This Is Where Your Life Truly Begins

This is the beginning. This path delivers. It is not easy. It will test you. It will break you. But it will also rebuild you. And on the other side of this battle is everything you have ever wanted.

Maybe you're leaving law school to become an actor. Maybe you've walked out of a corporate office with nothing but a whisper in your chest. Maybe you've quit medicine, marriage, ministry, or having motherhood as your only identity because something deeper was *calling.*

Whatever it looked like for you, the details are different, but the choice is the same. You've chosen **you.** You've stopped living someone else's version of your life. You've stopped shrinking to keep the peace. You've stopped apologising for wanting more.

Not everyone will understand. But your soul does. And now you're here, ready to write the story you were always meant to live.

So, let's fight this fight. Let's bury the old beliefs. Let's step into what we were born for.

This is where the real journey begins. This is holy ground.

Whatever has brought you to this place, you are welcome here.

◇◇◇◇◇

Chapter Summary

This chapter is about the brave choice to break free from the life that no longer fits. It's the raw, uncomfortable in-between, where old beliefs fight back and fear gets loud. You may feel guilt, doubt, and pressure to return to what's familiar, but your soul knows the truth: you can't stay where you no longer belong. Whether you left a career, relationship, or identity, this is the beginning of your true path.

◇◇◇

Soul Reflection Questions

1. What old beliefs or expectations have I been holding onto that no longer serve me, and how do they impact my ability to follow my path?

2. When was the last time I felt the pull of my true passion or purpose, and what would it take for me to fully embrace it?

3. What am I afraid to lose by following my true voice, and how can I reframe those fears to empower my journey?

4. What does true freedom look like to me, and how can I begin to release the fears and doubts that are holding me back from living it?

5. How can I honour my soul's calling while facing the inevitable struggles that come with breaking away from old patterns and beliefs?

CHAPTER FIVE

THE DEATH OF
THE OLD BELIEF

Round One: The Old Belief Throws the First Punch

Picture a boxing ring. You're in the center. Gloves on. Heart racing.

Across from you stands an old belief. One you didn't know you'd have to fight. It knows your fears. It knows your past. It knows exactly how to land the first blow.

Maybe yours sounds like:

- You're unlovable.
- You'll never recover from this.
- What happened to you is who you are.
- You don't get to rise.

For me, it was **Black Africans only belong in subservient roles. Dreaming is for others.**

When I walked into my first Australian university class to study filmmaking and journalism, I froze. I didn't see anyone who looked like me. And suddenly, my old belief stepped into the ring. Smirking. Looming.

You don't belong here, it hissed. **You're just playing dress-up. Turn back while you can.**

And maybe that's where you are right now.
You've stepped into unfamiliar territory—whether that's healing, creating, starting again, or just surviving. And just when you thought you were ready to rise, the old belief punches you. Hard.

I wanted to run.
I wanted to disappear.
But something deeper whispered: **stay.**

Round Two: The Old Belief Hits Harder

You thought you'd survived the worst. You stayed. You didn't run. And then the old belief comes back swinging. Harder. Sharper. More personal.

It says:

- **You think you're healed? Prove it.**
- **You think someone will love you after this? I don't.**
- **You think this business, this story, this dream will matter?**

For me, it came as rejection. Isolation. Racism. Being overlooked. Being silenced.

There were group assignments in film school.

Everyone partnered up—except me.
Over and over, I was left standing alone.
Invisible.
I'd go home and cry.
Not because I lacked talent, but because I believed the lie that I was too different.
Too **Black.**
Too **foreign.**
Too **unworthy** to belong.

I started hiding my hair.
Hiding my voice.
Hiding **me**.
Not because I wanted to, but because I thought I **had** to.
I was in survival mode, doing everything I could just to make it through.
The goal was to wake up, breathe, and get through the day.

Even in the fire, even under the weight of everything crumbling, some part of me kept walking. I couldn't live like this anymore. I had to find a way to live my **passion**, even though I didn't know how. I couldn't see the road, but something whispered **keep going.**

Without knowing it, I was on the journey of reclaiming my *true voice.*

Round Three: The Final Test—Losing Everything

There's a moment in every great story where the hero has fought. They've endured. They've dared to believe. And just when they think they've given all they could, life delivers a brutal blow.

It could be a **grief** so heavy, it suffocates every breath. You stand at a gravesite, watching the one you love being lowered into the earth. The world keeps spinning, cars keep moving, people keep laughing... and you just want to scream.

For others, it's a divorce that rips your world to shreds. The kids you once tucked into bed are no longer with you. The home you built, filled with memories and warm Sunday mornings, now belongs to someone else. You're left with echoes of laughter. Of a life you were sure would last. Of a love you thought was forever.

Then there's the one who followed the voice within. Walked away from a job, a salary, a title, a reputation, because their soul whispered **that they were made for more.** And now they sit in the dark at three a.m., bills unpaid, fridge empty, bank account bled dry, wondering if they just made the dumbest mistake of their life.

Some are watching their **dream slip through their fingers.** They did everything right—studied hard, worked hard, kept pushing hard—but somehow, they're still overlooked. Still unseen. Still stuck. They stare at a wall of rejection letters wondering if **it was all for nothing.**

And for others, it's a **health crisis.** You think you're fine, even as your body betrays you. Doctors speak in code, your strength disappears, and you watch your independence crumble.

You're no longer who you were. You're not sure who you'll become.

Maybe your **faith is gone.** You used to believe in something bigger. You used to feel connected. Now, the heavens are locked, and your prayers hit the ceiling and fall back into your lap like dust.

Maybe it's **everything at once.** You're raising kids alone. Your career is a warzone. Your friendships have disappeared. Your heart is broken. Your identity is a memory. You look in the mirror and don't recognise who's staring back. You wonder if you've failed. If you've gone too far. If there's still a way forward.

You've hit **rock bottom.** This is the pit. This is where *transformation* **actually** begins.

Because what gets stripped from you in Round Three is **everything that isn't real.** Everything that's not rooted in truth. Everything you thought made you worthy is gone. So you can finally rise with what **actually** lifts you up.

Round Three isn't the end. It's the place where false identities die, and real voices are born. It's where we don't just learn to survive. We learn to **rise.**

For me, Round Three looked like this:

- I was pregnant with my second child.
- My husband lost his job.
- He became an alcoholic, and I became his punching bag.
- I was kicked out of my home.
- My mother was in the hospital.
- I wasn't finished with university but I had no idea how I was going to pay my fees.

This was my battlefield. This was the point of no return. My filmmaking degree felt like a luxury I could no longer afford.

And then came the whisper, **you should've known better than to dream.**

I believed it. I didn't argue. I didn't fight back.
I packed my bags and went back to my home country.

The Moment of Truth

That trip home changed everything.

The moment I stepped off the plane and breathed in the air of my homeland, something cracked open in me. Surrounded by a sea of black African faces, I felt something I hadn't felt in a long time: **freedom.**

Freedom to speak without shrinking my accent.
Freedom to laugh loud. To walk proud. To be fully me.
Freedom to exist without apology.

And that's when I realised that I had been imprisoned. Not by chains, but by silence. By a system that asked me to erase myself just to belong. In trying to chase my **passion**, I had lost my identity. I had been trying to be a storyteller in a language that didn't support my soul. I had walked away from the lie, but I hadn't fully stepped into my truth.

I had embraced my gift, but not my roots.
I had found my voice, but not my **true** *voice*.

And here's the truth: You can't rise with half of your power.
You can't conquer with only your skills and none of your story.
You can't step into purpose while hiding parts of your soul.

The Shift

When I reconnected with my roots, everything changed. I studied the richness of Africa. I dove deep into our history, our power, our resilience. And in that *remembering*, I found the missing piece.

I came back to Australia with more than a story. I came back whole.

I wrote from that wholeness. I created from that place. And **I'm Not a Nurse** was born. A story that wasn't just a film, but a declaration. Funding followed. Doors opened. My voice—**my true voice**—echoed in rooms that once told me I didn't belong.

You might be there right now. You might feel like you've lost everything. Like your heart can't take another hit. The grief is too much. The betrayal too deep. The road ahead too foggy. The old belief will fight for its life. It'll scream that you're not enough. That you should settle. That you should shrink.

But hear me: **this is not the end.** This is the test before your awakening. The fire you're walking through is not to burn you down. It's to strip away everything that is not you, so only the real and the powerful remains. Let it burn off the lies. Let it shape your voice. You will realise you can't unsee what you've seen. You can't unlearn who you are *becoming*. You can't go back.

This is your cross. This is the weight you were born to carry—not as punishment, but as initiation. You may feel abandoned. Mocked. Bruised. But even in the darkest hour, know that

resurrection is coming. The old belief **must** die, so the true self can rise.

Keep walking. Even with shaky legs. Even with a broken heart. Even when no one claps, take the hits. Keep standing. As Rocky Balboa says, **you got to go through to get to where you want to get.**

◇◇◇◇◇

Chapter Summary

In the fire of pain, loss, and disillusionment, we are stripped of every false identity that once kept us small. The voices of doubt, shame, and survival may scream louder than ever, but it is now that the truth begins to rise. This fire is the birthplace of your *true voice*. So, take the hits. Stay in the ring. Let the old belief die, and let your soul *remember* who you were born to be.

◇◇◇

Soul Reflection Questions

1. What is the old belief that has followed you into every new beginning?

2. What moment in your life felt like a final blow—but actually marked the beginning of your *becoming*?

3. What parts of yourself have you silenced in order to be accepted?

4. When was the first time you felt you had to shrink in order to survive?

5. Have you mistaken your pain for punishment? What if it's actually your *portal*?

6. Who or what has been a mentor in your journey—seen or unseen?

7. What would it look like to carry your cross as your birthright?

8. If you stopped fighting for your limitations, what kind of life would you create?

9. Where are you still hiding your *true voice*, and why?

10. What truth is trying to rise from the ashes of your current fire?

THE AWAKENING

This is the moment you hear your soul clearly. A rising from the ashes. You begin to move with intention, connect to your calling, and recognise your power.

Chapters

◇ **Your Destined Throne**—Claim your divine seat of power and understand that your life has always been leading here.

◇ **The Birth of a New Belief**—Clearly see the pain within your path so that you can find forgiveness, healing, and love.

◇ **Rewriting the Narrative**—Shift your story from victim to visionary and create a powerful new internal dialogue.

◇ **The Call to Purpose**—Recognise what your purpose feels like, how it speaks to you, and how to say yes to it.

◇ **The Test Before the Take**—Understand the inevitable tests that come before stepping fully into alignment and how they strengthen you.

CHAPTER SIX

YOUR DESTINED THRONE

Let's stop. Breathe. Recognise where you are right now. Because something in you has shifted. You walked through fire. You held onto your dreams when everything told you to let go. You found a voice buried in silence and dared to speak again.

It's about honouring this sacred ground you now stand on.

What Is the Throne?

The *throne* is a spiritual position. An energetic seat. A soul-level recognition. The throne is your *inner authority*. It's the moment you no longer wait for someone else to validate your voice. You're not checking if the world approves anymore. You're not asking for permission to be who you are. You're **here**. And whether you realise it or not, you've been **enthroned**.

This isn't just about healing. It's about what healing revealed in you. **Authority**. Even if you don't fully see it yet. Even if you still feel unqualified or unsure. None of that changes the truth: your life, your voice, and your journey has **earned** you this *throne*.

This throne is evidence that the process has worked. It's where your soul sits now.

This isn't the same you from Chapter One. This is the **rebuilt** version of you. You are sitting in a position of **spiritual clarity**. And though some people may not fully see it yet, others will.

A Moment to Honour

Let this chapter be the pause that says **look at where you are**. You are seated on the throne destined for you. Your voice carries weight because everything you've lived makes your words **true**.

This is a reflection of who you've become.

Think about Mufasa in **The Lion King**. When he reclaimed the Pridelands, he wasn't chasing a crown. He didn't campaign for leadership. He didn't walk up Pride Rock and declare himself the king. He simply fought for what was his, stepped into his truth, and restored balance to a land that had been stripped of it. And when the battle was over, the sky opened. The rain fell. And in that moment, without a single word, everyone **knew** the *throne* was his. He had **earned** it.

The same is true for you.

You don't become a leader because you **want** to be one. You don't become a leader because you post motivational quotes on Instagram or slap the letters C.E.O. in your bio. It sneaks up on you.

For me, it happened when I least expected it. I'd walk into rooms just trying to exist, and suddenly, people were introducing me as **a leading speaker for women**. Every time, I'd hear it and think, **Leader? Me? I didn't apply for that position.** I wasn't trying to be anyone's leader. I didn't even know what that meant. Half the time, I was still figuring how to lead myself.

But it didn't matter what I thought. The people around me **saw** the battles I had fought, the obstacles I had overcome, the way I carried myself despite everything I had been through. And that's when it hit me. This wasn't a mistake or flattery. These moments were **signposts**. The universe, my ancestors, God—whatever you want to call it—was handing me the map to my next destination.

Because when I walked through the fire and survived, I didn't just walk away. I became ready to lead others through it.

People might say, **You inspire me. Your story moved me. I see something in you.** Don't brush it off. Don't downplay it. Don't shrink. Pay attention. Because those words aren't just compliments.

They are **confirmation.**

What Does It Mean to Lead?

So, what does it mean to take your place on this *throne*?

It means you're here to lead, but not necessarily in the way you might think. Leadership isn't just about titles, power, or authority. It's about impact. It's about guiding others, inspiring and showing them that they too can rise above their **pain** and claim their purpose. You have made it out of the pit and you are about to throw down the ladder for others to climb up.

On your throne, you're not just leading people from a place of position or power. You're leading from a place of empathy, understanding, love, and experience.

You understand struggle. You understand resilience. You understand the road to healing. And your leadership is grounded in the wisdom you've gained through your own journey. But here's the thing—there's a deeper call. A calling to create a **legacy** that impacts the people you lead directly and ripples through generations to come.

When you take your *throne*, it's also for everyone who comes after you. It's for those who will walk the path you've paved. You've broken the chains, and now it's time to help others do the same.

You are a warrior with a purpose. And that purpose is to change the world, starting with the people closest to you.

The Leader Was Always You

It is important for you to know that you were born a leader, with full authorship over your own life.

Inside you lives a compass, ancient and unshakable. A knowing that predates your fears, your traumas, even your name. You came here full of the wisdom, power, and clarity required to navigate your own *becoming*.

Life hands you a mirror. It reflects your light back to you, until you can finally see it for yourself. And for many, it takes years— sometimes decades—to see what was there all along.

You are not broken. You do not need fixing. What you need is *remembering*. You were never meant to outsource your power, your truth, or your purpose. This is the sacred work of life: to return inward, again and again, until you *remember* who you are beneath all the noise.

You are spirit wrapped in skin. Which means everything you need for this life—your path, your peace, your power—already lives within you. You are your own sanctuary. You are your own oracle. But until you awaken to this inner truth, you'll keep looking to others to lead you when you were born to lead yourself.

And here's the paradox: **we cannot fully guide others until we trust our ability to guide ourselves.**

This is your invitation to surrender. Not in weakness, but in reverence. Bow to the quiet power that lives in your soul. Because once you **truly** trust it, nothing outside of you can shake what you know to be true.

You understand struggle. You understand resilience. You understand the road to healing. You are the leader you've been waiting for. Your leadership is grounded in the wisdom you've gained through your own journey.

Now lead.

◇◇◇◇◇

Chapter Summary

Every heartbreak, every silence, every challenging moment shaped you into someone who no longer waits for permission to speak, lead, or live aligned. Your *throne* is about embodiment. It's the evidence that your pain had purpose and your voice holds authority because of who you've become. You've returned to your essence.

◇◇◇

Soul Reflection Questions

1. What pain did I once try to escape that now feels like a sacred teacher?

2. What part of me had to die for this version of me to be born?

3. How have I been unknowingly leading others just by surviving and showing up?

4. What does my *throne* look like—not externally, but internally?

5. What truth within me have I been afraid to speak, and why?

6. Where in my life am I still waiting for permission to rise?

7. How can I begin to honour the authority my journey has already given me?

8. What would it look like to lead my life from within rather than from expectation?

9. In what ways have I already been chosen—and how can I now choose myself fully?

10. What **legacy** am I here to build through the lessons I've lived?

CHAPTER SEVEN

THE BIRTH OF THE NEW BELIEF

Welcome to Your New World.

This moment is part of the plan your soul made long before you were born. Back in Chapter One, we talked about how the soul, before entering this life, chose everything with purpose: your parents, your environment, the joys and the pain; all of it was designed to shape you for a *mission* it could feel but not yet name.

And now, you've arrived at that sacred place. A quiet turning point.

This is the soul's next destination. It may not look like a grand moment. You might be tired, unsure, or even heartbroken. But this quiet space after the storm is the arrival point. The place your soul has been moving toward all along.

Think of it like graduating from a course you didn't even realise you were enrolled in.

All the lessons—grief, loss, betrayal, longing, illness, divorce, failure—they were part of your curriculum. The soul has been learning through every experience, even the painful ones. Especially the painful ones.

You might have gotten here through a breakup, a loss, a breakdown, or just an inner ache that wouldn't go away. It doesn't matter what brought you here.

What matters is that **you made it.**

This moment is holy.
It's the space between who you were and who you're *becoming.*
The old story is ending. The new story is just beginning.
You're in the in-between.

The part of you that was shaped by fear, survival, and people-pleasing is gently releasing its grip. It served you. It protected you. But now, it's time to let something deeper lead.

What's being born here are new beliefs. Truths your soul has always known.

- That you are not an accident.
- That your pain was not wasted.
- That your voice matters.
- That your journey has been preparing you all along.

This belief isn't something you learn, it's something you *remember.* It's always been inside you.

Check out the Set Up for My Story

The Warning of the White Man's Power

My soul chose to land in a world that would teach me to fear the power of the White man, knowing that one day I would face this power, their structures, their rules, and their biases. I was going to have to fight for my voice, for my right to tell stories that mattered, and for the rights of silenced voices.

A Passion for Storytelling

I was born with a *calling* to tell stories. Little did I know, the world around me would try to suppress this **passion** from the start.

Landing in the White Man's Land

Australia, a land my ancestors could never have imagined reaching, became the place I would plant my feet. It was a land that promised opportunity, but with it came the reality of living in a space where people like me were often invisible. The freedom I thought I would find was quickly overshadowed by the unspoken truth: I was welcome, but my **passion** was not.

The Fight for My Passion

Despite the welcoming words, I was told in more ways than one that my dreams were too big, my ambitions too bold. As an African-Australian woman, I wasn't supposed to be a creator. I was supposed to fit into a box, a role that society deemed appropriate for me. But my soul knew better. I was meant to thrive, to create, and to share my truth. I chose to reach for the forbidden fruit and fight for my dreams.

A Perfect Setup

The opposition I faced, the challenges placed in my way, were all part of the divine plan. The more resistance I met, the more my soul would rise. This was the fight I was born for—a fight to claim my voice, to prove that my **passion** was worth something, and that the *mission* of my soul would not be stopped.

Through this fight came my *gift*.

There I was, thinking I was merely navigating my journey, making decisions, charting my own course. Little did I know, I was but a character in a larger story, with a force far greater than myself pulling the strings. On the day I stumbled upon the title of my industry-funded film, **I'm Not a Nurse**, it was as though the universe had orchestrated this moment, guiding me through a plan I was yet to fully understand.

Let me tell you about **I'm Not a Nurse**. This film is a declaration of identity. It tells the story of a young African-Australian woman torn between societal expectations, familial obligations, and the pursuit of her filmmaking dreams. What began as a short film funded by Screenwest evolved into a book, both serving as profound reflections on identity, migration, and personal agency.

The title came to me in a moment of quiet reflection. I recall it vividly: I was walking through Piney Lakes Park, deep in thought about my journey as an African-Australian woman navigating an industry and a society that often tried to box me in. Unlike my usual approach of brainstorming endless title options, **I'm Not a Nurse** arrived as a singular, unwavering truth. And with that, a shift occurred. This title would go on to embody not only my personal struggles but a larger, universal story of identity and defiance.

This journey was about awakening to the truth that I was always meant to walk this path, to share this story, and to rise into the power of my true self.

When I first shared the title with my writing mentor, Miley Tunnecliffe, I expected the usual rounds of feedback and revisions. But instead, she smiled. A smile that said everything. **I'm Not a Nurse** resonated deeply, more than any title before it. It spoke to the collective experience of so many African-Australians and other marginalised groups whose aspirations and identities were often at odds with societal expectations.

As I began to write the script, I found myself confronting emotions I had buried for so long. This was more than a creative endeavour: it was an excavation of my soul. The tears I had kept hidden for years came rushing to the surface. In that moment, I realised this was a shared experience, one that echoed across cultures and communities. What began as my personal struggle soon blossomed into a universal conversation about identity, belonging, and the complexities of being African-Australian in a world that often didn't understand us. The resonance was undeniable. People would say it **felt like I was telling their story too.**

I had once thought that my desire to make films was a personal pursuit, just for me. But the truth is, I was standing up for many. In my hunger to share my story, I was giving voice to others who had been silenced.

I made **I'm Not a Nurse.** It travelled far. It won awards. But through it all, something deeper was rising within me. I was *becoming* something bolder, more confident, and undeniably powerful. There was a shift happening within me, an evolution that was the opposite of the woman I was when I first began. I no longer needed to prove anything, because somewhere along the way, I found the real me.

The Gift Inside Your Pain

For years, I chased a dream.

Looking back, I can see how ego played its part. It was all about me: my **passion**, my ambition, my name on the credits. I poured everything into that pursuit. And then something unexpected happened. Something I hadn't planned for.

I started noticing it, but only after others began to say it.

Strangers would stop me in the street, complimenting my bald head, my outfit, my **presence**. There was a light around me. I could feel it. And apparently, others could too:

You inspire me.
Your story feels like mine.
I love your courage and boldness.

I had put together a team of mostly White professionals, the kind of people I once thought would never listen to me. I had received funding, which I never thought was possible for someone who looked like me. I had made a film. But the real win?

I had become someone who no longer waited for permission.
I had become someone who dared to knock on doors I once feared.
I had learned to create **despite** the fear.
To show up fully, despite the doubts.

And that, right there, was the *gift* hidden inside the hustle. When I slowed down long enough to really see, it wasn't the success that changed me. It was the **pain** that came before it. The hard seasons. The quiet discrimination. The racism. The abuse. The self-doubt. The rejection letters. The moments I felt invisible in rooms where I had worked hard to belong. The tears I cried when no one was watching. That's where my courage was born. That's when my voice grew louder.

Transformation **is a soul contract.**

Before the healing comes the breaking. Before the clarity, the storm. Before the soul can rise,

it must first be burned to ashes by the very fire it came here to face. This is the journey. This is what *transformation* looks like. A sacred disruption that shakes the foundation you once called daily life.

A grief.
A loss.
An illness.
A betrayal.
A silence that suddenly swallows everything you thought you knew.

I once met a tattoo artist with a steady hand and a steady life. She had rhythm. She had routine. She had made sense of the world. Until the world stopped making sense. Her three-year-old daughter passed away. Suddenly. Without warning. Without reason. And her life split in two: **before** and **after**.

The pain was unspeakable. The kind that breaks the body, the breath, the will to exist.

What shattered her most was the silence that followed. There was no village for her. No support. No safe place to fall apart.

And in that unbearable silence, something began to stir. Questions rose like smoke inside her bones. **Why should any mother carry this kind of grief alone? Why is there no space for this kind of pain? Why does the world not make room for the howl of a broken mother's heart?**

Those questions became her teacher. That ache became her awakening. And slowly—through the ashes of what was—a *mission* began to form. It became about every mother who is made to grieve in the shadows. It became about building the very thing that didn't exist when she needed it most.

Today, she's creating sacred spaces for grieving mothers. This is what it looks like when your deepest heartbreak becomes your highest purpose. This is what it means to rise with the *gift* you were always meant to carry.

I told her what I deeply believe: **You and your daughter made this agreement before you arrived here.** Your soul, and her soul, knew the cost. And you both agreed to it because your spirit is strong. Your daughter knew you would carry a torch to light the path for others.

She began to connect the dots. She's a builder. A doer. The kind of woman who moves mountains when she believes in something. This wasn't the end. It was the sacred beginning. An unravelling designed to shake loose the truth that was always there. And right there in that café, while our words spilled across a white table, a soft light appeared: a rainbow resting between our mugs, like a quiet blessing. As goosebumps danced on our arms, she whispered through tears: **Rainbow was my daughter's favourite colour.**

YOUR TRUE VOICE ✦ JESSICA BAILEY

Often, the very thing that shatters us is the very thing we came to heal.

Meeting this woman, just like so many others that I have met, felt like **destiny disguised as devastation**. And in that moment, she began to live her *mission*.

Turn Your Weakness into an Advantage

In the movie *Unstoppable*, based on the true story of Anthony Robles, we witness the powerful *transformation* of one man who became the opposite of the belief he was born into.

Anthony entered the world with one leg. From the beginning, society handed him a script filled with limitations. He was expected to live small, to stay on the sidelines, to accept that having one leg would define him. The belief system said: **You're not enough.** But Anthony didn't just defy that belief, he lived to contradict it.

He chose wrestling, a sport built on balance, strength, and leverage—all things which the world said he lacked. He was stepping into a ring at the same time as he was stepping into a fight against every label he'd been given. With grit, discipline, and faith, he rewrote the narrative. He trained harder. He worked longer. He turned what others saw as a weakness into unmatched advantage.

Eventually, Anthony became an NCAA Wrestling Champion, and was undefeated in his final season. He had one leg and he was unstoppable. He became a champion wrestler and a powerful motivational speaker. After winning the NCAA Wrestling Championship, Anthony walked away with his medals and his message. Where the world saw limitation, Anthony saw purpose.

He now travels the globe as a speaker, sharing his story with audiences ranging from students to CEOs. He speaks about resilience, mindset, perseverance, and turning perceived weaknesses into strengths. He took the belief system that once told him he wasn't enough, and used it as fuel to inspire others, reminding people that their greatest challenges can become their greatest power.

Anthony Robles went from underestimated to **unstoppable**.

How to Spot the Gift Inside Your Pain

We all inherit a belief opposite to the one we are here to teach. **This is the moment when you find out what that opposite is for you.**

If you have made it this far, if you have fought your battle, if you have crawled out of the fire, then guess what? Your **pain** has left you with a *gift*.

It's time to claim it.

Step 1: Ask Yourself What Shifted.

- What is something I can do now that I couldn't before?
- What part of me feels stronger, wiser, or more confident?

Step 2: Identify the Old Belief That Died.

- What belief kept me stuck before?
- How do I know it no longer has power over me?

Step 3: Recognise the New Belief That Was Born.

- If today were my last day, what truth would I want to leave with the world?
- How does this truth make me feel?

Step 4: Own It.

- How will I show up differently in my life?
- How will I use this gift moving forward?

What Happens When You Spot the Gift in Your Pain?

Pain can feel cruel. These struggles that we go through can feel like a punishment, like something unfair that life threw at you with no explanation. But when you step back and really **look,** you start to see something else.

The moment you recognise the *gift* your pain left behind, something shifts. You stop seeing yourself as a victim of life and start to see yourself as someone **chosen** for something greater.

1. You Release Resentment.

The people who hurt you were not the reason you suffered. Yes, they played a role. Yes, they caused you **pain**. But they were simply the *collaborators*. The real suffering came from not understanding **why** it was happening. This would allow you to realise that you were all working together. Your soul made a deal with them. When I realised my **pain** was planned, that it was carefully orchestrated and had led me to my purpose, I stopped thinking of who I could blame for it. I stopped hating my ex who was abusive to me. I stopped resenting the racism I experienced. I stopped being angry at life for being unfair. Because without those struggles, I wouldn't be who I am today.

They were my collaborators.

Every story needs characters to push the plot forward. Now, I could give them a handshake for a job well executed. They offered exactly what I wanted and pushed me exactly where I wanted to be.

Now, let's be clear—this is **not** about excusing what happened.

It's about seeing that they were just doing their job, by *shaping me* into the person I was always meant to become. And when I understood that, forgiveness became easy.

We cannot move forward while carrying the weight of bitterness.

2. You Heal.

Pain holds power over you when you don't know what to do with it. When you think suffering is pointless, it keeps you trapped. It makes you afraid.

But the moment you find the *gift* in your pain, healing begins. Suffering is no longer just suffering. Now, it's *a lesson.* And just like that, the wound stops being a wound. It becomes **wisdom.**

3. You Open the Door for Love.

When you're carrying **pain**, you might not even realise how much it blocks love. When you're bitter, you push people away. When you're full of resentment, you close yourself off.

When you release it, **love rushes in.**

You start attracting people who reflect your new belief system. You start experiencing relationships in a deeper, truer way. You stop fearing love because **pain** no longer defines you. You become open. You become whole. You become *ready.*

And most importantly, you open up for your soul to tell you more about this adventurous journey it has orchestrated.

4. You Step into Your Purpose

Now, you have a *calling.* You have something to share. Something to teach. The more you surrender to soul, the more the soul shows you.

Pain Did Not Break You

Right now, you stand at the edge of a new reality. You don't have to carry anger anymore. You don't have to keep questioning why it happened. You have your answer.

It happened to **shape you.** Now, you are strong and the world needs what you have gained. So take the *gift.* And get ready to use it.

This is the birth of your new belief. A belief not rooted in fear, pressure, or performance, but in soul. A belief that whispers:

- I am here on purpose.
- Nothing has been wasted.
- My journey is sacred.
- I am not too late.
- I am *becoming*.

You've crossed through the darkness. You've done the inner work. Now, a new whisper is *calling*. Prepare for a new beginning.

◇◇◇◇◇

Chapter Summary

This is not the end, but the divine beginning—the moment your old belief dies, and your new belief is born. One that says: **I am not broken. I was** becoming. **And now, I rise—whole, worthy, and ready to lead with the light.**

◇◇◇

Soul Reflection Questions

1. What painful experience in my life keeps returning to my thoughts, asking to be seen differently?

2. What belief about myself did I carry before the pain, and how has that belief shifted now?

3. Can I name the new truth that has emerged from my darkest moment?

4. In what ways did my pain break me open, and what beauty came through the cracks?

5. What gifts, strengths, or wisdoms do I hold because of what I've been through?

6. What old patterns or roles am I now ready to release in order to become more of who I really am?

7. Who or what am I being invited to forgive for my own liberation?

8. Where in my life have I been waiting for permission— and how can I now give it to myself?

9. How is my story meant to serve others, and who might be waiting for me to rise and speak it?

10. If my pain was a sacred agreement my soul made, what was it trying to awaken me to?

CHAPTER EIGHT

REWRITING THE NARRATIVE

You see it now. This voice you've uncovered is now also a guiding light for others.

Because here's the truth: for a voice to **carry,** to **move nations,** to **shift atmospheres,** it must sit in a place of **authority.** You've earned yours. Now the question becomes **what are you going to do with it?**

What do you do with the power you've reclaimed? What do you do now that you've *remembered* who you really are? **You rewrite the narrative.**

Until now, your life was shaped by stories that didn't belong to you. Stories passed down, spoken and unspoken. Stories written in fear, shame, scarcity, trauma. Stories that told you how to survive, but did not teach you how to thrive.

Now you know better. And you're about to do something radical. You are about to write a new story for yourself and for everyone who is still stuck in their old one.

A coaching client of mine messaged me one day with a story that cracked something open in both of us. She had just begun to reconnect with her own voice, to write her truth, and reclaim a part of herself that had long been silenced.

But what she didn't expect was that her healing journey would uncover an even older silence—one that belonged to her mother.

She said, 'Jess, I just spoke to my mum. She said that when she was little, the youngest of five, she played cowboys and Indians with her brothers. But she was only allowed to be the nurse.'

She was shocked by how deeply it mirrored her own life. How the same script that caged her voice had once bound her mother. And as she dug deeper, more truths emerged. More silences. More limits.

The realisation hit her hard: this was generational. She was rewriting the story for all the women before her who never got the chance. This is the nature of the *soul's plan*. We come to break cycles, not just live through them. We come to be the ones who say **enough**.

Your old belief system was a **generational curse** that has suffocated many before you, and is still suffocating others now. You are the one who gets to break it, rewrite it, and teach **the old version of you**. This was why you came: to break old curse, set caged voices free, and bring freedom. Jesus died on the cross so that the sins of the world would be washed away. You are the same.

There are others out there who are still in the same place as that younger version of yourself; still trapped in fear, doubt, and limiting beliefs, thinking they have to play small, that success isn't for **people like them**. Now that **you know better**, you can be the hero they need to help to rewrite their story. You are the one reaching back to say: **I've been where you are. Take my hand. Let me show you the way.** This is your purpose, revealed as the opposite of your inherited beliefs.

Your **pain** trained you for something. It handed you a responsibility. Now, it's time to use it. Until now, you've been living within a script written by others. But now? You are the author. The pen is in your hands, and you alone decide how the story unfolds from here.

Step 1: Identify the Old Narrative You Are Here to Rewrite.

Before you can rewrite anything, you have to know what you're rewriting.

So pause.
Close your eyes, if you need to.
Feel into your past.

Ask yourself:

- What was the lie I believed for far too long?
- What belief shaped my choices, my confidence, my sense of worth?
- Whose voice did I internalise that told me I was too much or not enough?
- What story did I tell myself when I didn't fit in? When I was rejected? When I failed?

These aren't just thoughts. They're narratives. They are inherited, embedded, repeated.

It's time to rewrite them.

Step 2: Know Who You Are Rewriting For.

Now that you've named the lie, it's time to name the people still trapped in it.

Who are you here to help? Who needs your story?

Your message is for a specific someone who needs what your journey has revealed. Someone out there is still stuck in the place you've walked through and risen from.

For me, the lie was this: power belongs to people who are White, male, confident, and privileged. I didn't see people like me in positions of power. I thought I didn't belong.

But after walking through **pain** and rising up anyway, I found a deeper truth: power is not exclusive. There is a *throne* for everyone.

That became the message. And now, I speak to those who've been made to feel small, invisible, or unworthy of leadership. To the woman told to stay in her place. To the people who have never seen someone like them in charge. To those shrinking in front of groups they were born to lead.

Now, ask yourself:

- ✦ Who is still where I used to be?
- ✦ What parts of themselves would they see in my old story?
- ✦ How can I help them believe in their own power?

This is about purpose. You're doing it for the ones who are still stuck. Write for them.

Step 3: Define Your New Narrative.

This is the truth you carry. The message you were born to tell. Now that you've exposed the old belief and identified the people who need your message, it's time to write the *truth* you are bringing into the light. This is your new narrative.

It's the truth your life now represents. The message you want to repeat until the walls fall down. The new idea that challenges the old lie and sets others free.

Ask yourself:

- What truth do I know now that others haven't discovered yet?
- What message do I want to become known for?
- What belief, if someone **truly** accepted it, would change their life?

Your new narrative should be:

- **Personal.** It comes from your journey, and you live it daily.
- **Disruptive.** It challenges the old pattern and shifts mindsets.
- **Clear.** One bold truth that cuts through others' confusion.

When I reflect on this, I think:

- **Old Belief:** 'I need to stay small to be accepted.'
- **New Narrative:** 'I was born to take up space, and I won't shrink for anyone.'
- **Old Belief:** 'Black people don't belong in power.'
- **New Narrative:** 'Power is claimed, and I'm here to claim mine.'

Now it's your turn:

- What's the lie you once believed?
- Rewrite it into a powerful, soul-anchored truth.
- This becomes your **guiding message:** what you'll say, teach, and embody.

Step 4: Share Your Story

You've named the lie. You've found your people. You've written your new truth. Now ask yourself: what got you here? What was the exact thing you used to break through?

- Look closely: what did you **do** that changed everything?
- What mindset, tool, habit, belief, or action helped you rise?
- Write it down. This is your new story.

This is what your people need to know. It's the missing piece in their journey—the knowledge they don't yet have. And you're going to guide them through it. Let them know that their **story may look different, but they apply themselves, they will find their way to a throne too.**

You Are the Rewrite

The pain you survived and the wisdom you have gained led you here. Now, you are not just breaking free for yourself. You are breaking free so that others can follow. Live the truth. Spread the message. And rewrite the story—for you and for them.

◇◇◇◇◇

Chapter Summary

You are the author now. You are writing a new story for yourself and for every silenced voice, every wounded ancestor, and every future soul who needs to know that freedom is possible. You carry a sacred responsibility to rewrite and liberate.

◇◇◇

Soul Reflection Questions

1. What lie about yourself or your worth have you carried the longest, and where did it come from?

2. How has that lie shaped your decisions, your voice, and the way you've shown up in the world?

3. Whose voice did you mistake for your own, and what has reclaiming your true voice revealed?

4. What old story are you ready to release, and what truth are you ready to live instead?

5. If your story could liberate just one person, who would you want it to reach and why?

6. Who is still trapped in the same narrative you've broken free from?

7. What message do you now carry that has the power to disrupt generational patterns?

8. How does your new narrative challenge systems of fear, shame, or scarcity that once held you back?

9. What tool, belief, or breakthrough helped you reclaim your *throne* and how can you offer it to others?

10. If your life became a living message of hope, what would it say to the world?

CHAPTER NINE

THE CALL TO PURPOSE

The Shift From Self to Service

At the beginning of this journey, it was about survival. You were fighting to break free from the chains of old beliefs, stepping into your *true voice*, your power, and discovering what you were truly capable of. But now, a deeper truth emerges. True fulfillment comes from how you use your evolution to elevate others.

This is why the greatest leaders, thinkers, and creators create movements.

- They don't just build wealth; they **build opportunities.**
- They don't just find their voice; they **amplify other voices.**
- They don't just heal themselves; they *become a source of* **healing for others.**

This is the moment where everything you have fought for takes on a greater purpose.

This Is the Hardest Transformation

If you thought breaking your old belief was hard, and stepping into your power was a challenge, then this next stage will demand even more from you. Because now, you are also carrying others.

The final evolution is when you take everything you have learned, every battle you have won, every demon you have slain, and you use it for something greater than yourself.

This is the chapter where your growth stops being personal and starts being **legacy**. Shift your story from victim to visionary and create a powerful new internal dialogue.

And that means:

- You will be tested in new ways.
- You will be called to step up when it's inconvenient.
- You will have to stretch beyond your comfort zone for those who need you.

This is why many stop growing once they achieve personal success. Leading others is a responsibility. But you didn't come this far to stop now.

Stepping Into Your Purpose

You feel the undeniable knowing that you weren't meant to just survive, but to create, make an impact, and leave something behind that matters.

Step One: Acknowledge That Something New is Calling And Surrender to It

You won't have all the answers. It will feel uncertain. You may even doubt yourself. Step forward anyway. Say yes before you have the full picture. Say yes before you feel ready. It's about trust. The same force that led you through your battles is the same force still leading you now.

Your only job is to follow it.

Step Two: Exploring the Suitable Channels To Serve

Now it's time to create a strategy. Because **purpose without action is just a dream.**

Will you...

- Start a brand to spread your message?
- Write a book? Speak on stages? Mentor others?
- Launch a charity or foundation to serve your cause?
- Work with an organisation that aligns with your *mission*?

This is the moment to make your purpose tangible. To take it from something you understand to something you do.

Step Three: Seek Guidance
No one gets to the top alone.

Find mentors. Find those who have walked this path before you. Learn from their experiences. It's not about copying someone else's journey, but accepting their wisdom to inform your own. Be humble enough to ask for help. Be open enough to receive it.

There is strength in seeking and receiving guidance.

Step Four: Following the Call, Even When It Scares You
When I first realised that I carried **an** ability to inspire, I didn't know what to do with it. I wasn't a speaker. I wasn't a coach. I was just an African-Australian woman who had passed through the fire.

Then life sent me a guide who had seen the inspirational social media clips I posted whenever I **felt like it.** She looked at me and said, **Jessica, let's brand you. You were meant for this.** She wanted to mentor me, to turn me into a guide for others. And I freaked out. This wasn't my world. What would people say if I **abandoned** filmmaking—the thing I said I was passionate about? I mean, this whole fight was to live my **passion,** and now I'm saying something else is *calling*?

I didn't even know anything about coaching, I couldn't even get my own shit together. I didn't think I was qualified to guide someone else. What if I failed? Who would trust a 30-year-old woman to guide them in their journey? And the **cost for this**

woman to help me meant emptying my bank account. It was scary.

Everything in me wanted to run.
But I didn't.
I leaned into the fear. I took the step. I gave it a go.
And I have never looked back.

Now, I am a certified life coach, speaking on stages, guiding people worldwide. Now, I see the truth so clearly: the *calling* was always there. Film was never **the** thing. It was just a vehicle to get me here.

Your calling may not make sense at first. It will feel uncomfortable. It will challenge your identity. It will make you question everything. But if you ignore it, you will always feel that something is missing.

Ask yourself:

- ✦ What is life inviting you into right now?
- ✦ What opportunity, idea, or shift has been on your heart, but you keep resisting?
- ✦ If fear wasn't a factor, what would you step into today?

Step Five: Brace for Resistance
Stepping into your purpose is exhilarating, but it also comes with a cost. Not everyone will cheer you on. Not everyone will understand. And that's something you need to prepare for.

Growth unsettles people. When you begin to step into your true voice, those who knew the old version of you may struggle to accept your *transformation*. Some will doubt you. Some will gossip. Others will tell you you're making a mistake. And if you're not prepared, that resistance can shake you.

I know this because I lived it.

When I started pursuing my path, people around me whispered that I lacked focus. They laughed at me. Gossip spread. I heard it, I felt it. But I didn't stop.

And then, the day came. The first time I stepped on stage and delivered a keynote speech that really moved the room, I watched the same people who once doubted me change their tune. same people who once called me crazy were now telling me I was meant to be a speaker. But by then, I had already learned the truth.

No one else gets to define your path.

Your purpose wasn't assigned by society, by your family, or by the voices trying to keep you small. Your job is to listen; to trust the pull inside you, even when no one else does.

The resistance is part of the process. The doubt from others is proof that you're stepping outside the mould. But here's what you **must** do: **find your people.** Seek out those who see who you are *becoming*. Surround yourself with the ones who believe in you when the road gets tough.

Because when the world tells you to shrink, the right community will remind you to keep rising.

Step Six: Stand in Your Power, Even When Doubts Arise
As you move forward, you will encounter moments of self-doubt. You'll question whether you're on the right path. That's natural. But you have to stand firm.

Believe in your purpose. Believe in the path that has led you here. And believe in the power that has carried you through. You've earned your place.

Step Seven: Trust that You are Equipped for This
You might feel like you don't know enough. Like you're not **ready** to step into this next version of yourself. Let me tell you the truth: you already have everything you need. Your **pain** refined

you. Your struggles trained you. Your experiences have made you an expert.

For me, my **passion** for storytelling was never just about film, it was about understanding **narratives**, understanding **what makes a hero.** That knowledge is what I use now to guide others through their own story. Nothing has been wasted.

You don't need to wait until you feel ready. You don't need someone else's permission. Your purpose is calling now, and you are equipped. Ask yourself:

- What skills, experiences, or wisdom have your struggles given you?
- What do people already come to you for guidance on?
- How could those things be used to help others?

Step Eight: Taking the First Step (Even If It's Small)

Living your *mission* is not about having a **perfect plan**. It's about starting.

When I stepped into my *calling*, I didn't have it all figured out. I took the leap, and I learned along the way. And that's what you must do.

Your first step doesn't have to be big.

- It could be sharing your story for the first time.
- It could be applying for that thing you've been afraid of.
- It could be starting that business, that project, that movement that has been stirring inside you.
- It could be mentoring someone who needs your wisdom.

You don't have to see all the way to the top of the staircase. Just take the first step.

Your New Role Requires That You Do Something With It:

- **Speak it.** Share your story. Whether it's on social media, in conversations, or on stages, start spreading your message.

- **Build something from it.** This is how movements begin. Start a project, a brand, a business, or a platform that embodies this truth.

- **Teach it.** If you've broken free, help others do the same. Mentor, coach, create, lead.

- **Keep breaking the spell.** When you see someone trapped in the old belief, remind them of the truth. Be the person that *you once needed*.

Reflection Exercise:

- Who can you serve, help, or impact with what you've been given?

- What is one small action you can take today toward your purpose?

- What would happen if you just **started**?

You've been through the storm. You've survived the darkness. Now, step into the light. Your purpose is calling. Don't wait for permission. Don't wait for the perfect moment. The time is now.

◇◇◇◇◇

Chapter Summary

Every wound, every breakthrough, every chapter of your *becoming* was preparing you for your healing as someone else's hope. Your voice becomes a guide, and your life becomes **legacy**. Purpose is a decision to show up, again and again, for something greater than you. All that's left is to take action.

◇◇◇

Soul Reflection Questions

1. What deep inner knowing or restlessness have I been ignoring that might actually be my calling in disguise?

2. What voices from the past (family, culture, society) still try to define my path and what truth do I now choose instead?

3. Where in my life have I turned pain into wisdom and how could that wisdom serve someone else now?

4. Who do I feel called to help, speak to, or guide, and why might I be the perfect person for them?

5. What gifts or messages am I sitting on because I don't feel ready, and what if I already am?

6. If my story could speak, what would it say to someone who is where I used to be?

7. If fear wasn't in the way, what bold action would I take toward my greater purpose today?

8. When was the last time I felt fully alive, lit up, and aligned—and what was I doing?

9. Who are the people I need to surround myself with in this new season and what kind of support do I need?

10. What's one small step I can take this week to embody my purpose more boldly, even if it scares me?

CHAPTER TEN

THE TEST BEFORE
THE TAKE-OFF

You've done the hard work.

You've stepped into your purpose. You've chosen your platform, claimed your voice, your story, and your message. But it doesn't mean the journey gets easier.

Welcome to the Inner Battle.

You think the old beliefs are gone. And in a way, they are. But old beliefs don't die, they **evolve**. They're still hecklers sitting in the front row of your new life, they just have new masks.

- Self-doubt.
- Imposter syndrome.
- Fear of being seen.
- The voice that says, '**Who do you think you are? You? From that place? Why would anyone listen to you?**'

This is the quiet war between who you used to be and who you're *becoming*. It's what I call *the* **test before the take-off.**

Why So Many Quit Here

It's not because they don't have a message. Not because they're not gifted. But because they weren't ready for the resistance that shows up **after** clarity. They thought stepping into purpose would silence fear. It doesn't.

1. Old Beliefs Become New Voices of Doubt

They may sound different now, but it's the same old voices. They show up as hesitation, fear of failure, constant second-guessing, over-preparation, or procrastination. Here's the key: these voices are not your *true voice*. They are echoes of old programming. You have to learn to recognise and override them.

You are not going backward. You're just being tested.

2. Your Voice Is a Newborn—It Needs Time to Grow

Your voice is powerful. But it's also new. It's like a baby just learning to walk.

Don't expect it to run before it crawls.
Don't expect it to be fearless on day one.
Don't put it in the ring before it's ready.

Too many give up because they think their voice should be bulletproof straight away. Real power takes time. Protect your voice. Speak, even if your voice shakes. Feed it with your new truth. Practice, even when you're not sure anyone's listening. You're raising something sacred. Treat it that way.

3. Resistance Is Part of the Process

Every time you rise, something will try to pull you back.

The test before the take-off is here to prepare you. It strengthens your voice. It deepens your message. It lights up your soul. And if you pass this test—maybe not perfectly, but faithfully—you'll take off in a way that no one can deny.

4. It Will Take Time—And That's Okay

Your purpose isn't a microwave meal. It's a masterpiece.

That means patience. That means consistency. That means showing up even when it feels like no one is listening. Once you plant a seed, you **water it.** You **protect it.** You **give it time to grow.**

Your voice and your purpose are the same.

5. Adapt the Student Mindset

Confidence comes from **learning.** You don't have to be the best on day one, but you **do** have to commit to growth.

That's where most people fail. They step into their purpose, but they don't invest in it. They don't study it. They don't hone their craft. And then they wonder why they still feel like frauds.

What will help you master your voice? Reading? Training? Surrounding yourself with mentors? Practicing relentlessly? Whatever it is, throw yourself into it. Nothing you learn will go to waste, because you're going to carry this voice **for the rest of your life.**

When I realised that life coaching was the right channel for my purpose, I studied it. I trained. I learned how to refine my gift. I speak frequently on social media as a way of practicing my speaking skill. You must do the same.

Your voice is your *gift.*

Now, it's time to train it, protect it, and prepare it for the impact it was meant to make. This also helps you build confidence. The more you train your *true voice*, the more you master it, and the more you master it, the more confident you become.

◇◇◇◇◇

Chapter Summary

Stepping into purpose is beginning of a deeper battle. **The test before the take-off** is the sacred time where old doubts wear new masks, resistance shows up uninvited, and your newborn voice learns how to walk. The key is not to run from the test but to lean into it, train your voice like the *gift* it is, and trust that this is preparing you for a *take-off* that will change everything.

◇◇◇

Soul Reflection Questions

1. Where in my life do I still hear the voice of old beliefs dressed up as new doubt?

2. What does my inner battle look like right now, and how is it showing up in my journey?

3. When fear or imposter syndrome shows up, how do I usually respond, and how can I respond differently?

4. In what ways am I expecting my voice to be perfect instead of allowing it to grow as it needs to?

5. What am I currently resisting, and could that resistance actually be a sign that I'm close to something powerful?

6. Am I giving myself permission to be a student again? If not, why?

7. What kind of support, mentorship, or training do I need to confidently grow into my purpose?

8. How can I measure progress not by perfection, but by faithfulness to the process?

9. What sacred daily practice can I create to protect and nurture my voice?

10. If I fully believed that this test is preparing me for *take-off*, how would I show up differently today?

THE BECOMING

Here, you embody your truth. You step fully into your identity, own your story, and begin to show up with bold authenticity. Your voice becomes your compass.

Chapters

◇ **Your Uniqueness**—Identify the traits, patterns, and **passions** that make you unlike anyone else.

◇ **The Power of Your Voice**—Learn how to use your voice to lead, heal, and resonate deeply with others.

◇ **The Power of Your Design**—Dive into how you move through the world and serve with ease.

◇ **The Power of Your Story**—Understand your story as a healing, inspiring force and learn how to share it with impact.

◇ **You as a Brand**—Begin to see yourself as a living, breathing brand that carries a message, energy, and **legacy**.

◇ **The Circle of Mirrors**—Reflect on how your relationships, community, and environment mirror your growth and truth.

CHAPTER ELEVEN

YOUR UNIQUENESS

Every purpose-driven person gets to this point. They've said yes to their calling, but start feeling small again when they hear the noise of the crowd. They wonder if their voice will just blend into the background. Something is beginning to whisper again:

- Others are already doing this.
- What makes **you** different?
- Who's going to choose **your** voice when there are so many out there?

It's the echo of old programming, but this time, it's wearing another mask. Now, it's about **why anyone should care.**

You wonder if maybe you should change it to sound more polished, like someone already known, and already successful.

Your Greatest Advantage Is What You've Been Taught to Hide

Most people believe that the truth alone is enough. They believe the message should speak for itself. And while it holds power, it needs something more to **connect with others.**

Your voice isn't just the truth you've discovered. It becomes **complete** when that truth flows **through your channel**—your **passions**, your talents, your quirks, your background, your energy. These are the language your people will understand. They're the texture that makes the truth tactile, relatable, and **undeniably yours.**

Think of your truth as your light. It's real. It's radiant. It's meant to be seen. But it needs a vessel; a stained-glass window through which it can shine. That's your personality. Your humour. Your cultural lens. Your rhythm. Your story. That's how your light becomes your art. That's how your voice becomes **a beacon.**

People look for truth in a form they can feel, understand, and receive. When you try to sound like someone else, you're putting your truth through someone else's *channel*, and your people won't hear you. But when you show up as the whole you? The flawed, brilliant, soulful, and sacred you? That's when your voice **awakens others.**

So stop trying to polish your edges until you disappear. Stop editing your essence to seem more professional or palatable. The truth you carry becomes *transformational* when it flows through the *channel* of your fully expressed life. **You just need to become more you.**

And that is what makes you **unforgettable.**

The World Needs You.

Let me show you how this plays out:

- The introverted coach who thought they weren't dynamic enough to lead built a six-figure business through deep listening and thoughtful presence, and their clients say no one's ever made them feel so seen.
- The woman who felt insecure about her thick accent became a powerful speaker, and her voice now stands as a symbol for other immigrants to rise.

- The young boy raised in a small rural town used his humble roots to write bestselling stories that connected with readers around the world.

- The Black woman who didn't see herself represented in leadership became the representation she needed, and now speaks on global stages from the fullness of who she **is**.

These people didn't need to be the most popular, most polished, or most perfect. They just needed to be themselves, unapologetically and consistently. And so do you.

Your uniqueness isn't separate from your purpose. It's the fuel for it.

The very things you thought you had to hide or forget are the keys to making your purpose impactful and unforgettable. Your uniqueness is in the *channel*. It's what makes you undeniable.

- **Your Personality.** How your natural rhythm, energy, and way of being can attract the right people and make lasting impact.

- **Your Identity.** How your culture, your roots, and your story bring richness to your message.

- **Your Experience.** How your pain, your victories, and even your silence have all been preparing you for your unique lane.

- **Your Voice.** How to speak in a way that cuts through the noise, touches hearts, and lingers long after you've finished.

- **Your Presence.** How to stop shrinking, start taking up space, and radiate the fullness of who you are.

You were born to stand out. Ground yourself in this truth. Because what's coming next is not about being more, it's about *becoming* fully you.

Your story is your blueprint.
Your uniqueness is in your *channel*.
Your life is your qualification.

And someone out there is waiting on **you** to show up and lead the way.

◇◇◇◇◇

Chapter Summary

The moment you begin to doubt your place in a crowded world is the exact moment you must anchor deeper into your uniqueness. You were called to embody your voice, your story, and your presence. The power of your purpose doesn't lie in being someone else; it lies in *becoming* fully, unapologetically **you**.

◇◇◇

Soul Reflection Questions

1. Where in my journey have I felt the urge to shrink, blend in, or copy others?

2. What parts of myself have I been hiding because I believed they made me less than others?

3. Who am I trying to impress, and is it costing me my authenticity?

4. Which aspects of my background or personality have I seen as weaknesses that might actually be my strengths?

5. What is the unique language or channel through which my truth flows most naturally?

6. What would it look like to show up fully as myself—without apology or edit?

7. What lies have I believed about needing to look or sound like others in order to succeed?

8. How can I honour my culture, quirks, **passions**, or lived experiences in the way I share my message?

9. What story, truth, or perspective do I carry that only I can express in the way I do?

10. What one bold step can I take this week to stop hiding and start owning my divine difference?

CHAPTER TWELVE

THE POWER OF YOUR VOICE

Now that you understand your unique mix of personality, identity, experiences, voice, and presence that no one else on this earth shares, it's time to clarify the one thing that brings it all together: your *true voice*.

Not your literal speaking voice or your tone and style, but the clear, grounded truth that you're here to express in your own way.

Why This Step Matters

You may already know your niche. Maybe you coach on confidence. Maybe you teach people how to reclaim their power. Or maybe you support others through grief, motherhood, business growth, health, or healing. That's great, but it's not enough.

Everyone is talking about success.
Everyone is talking about purpose.
Everyone is talking about healing.

If you don't get clear on **what part of the conversation you are uniquely meant to lead,** your voice gets lost in the noise. This is why so many people feel unseen on social media. Why the posts fall flat. Why the drive fizzles out. It's because they haven't found their unique **angle**.

Your voice is the *angle*. The unique lens. The binding thread that runs through all your content, offerings, and presence.

So how do you find your angle? By soul-searching. What did life teach you that you couldn't ignore, even when you tried? What's the message you find yourself coming back to, over and over again?

1. Start With the Bigger Picture

What is the broad area you're drawn to? Is it purpose? Healing? Confidence? Leadership? Motherhood? Identity? Success? Something else?

This is your arena. The stadium you've walked into. It's full of other voices, too. So, now we narrow it to yours.

2. What Specific Problem Do You Solve?

Don't overthink it. Start simple. Use this prompt: 'I help people ____ so they can ____ .'

Some examples:

- I help people redefine **success** so they can build a life that feels good on the inside.
- I help women reclaim their **identity** after motherhood so they can feel like themselves again.
- I help creatives turn their life stories into **impact**-driven brands.
- I help people find the **courage** to speak their truth, even when their voice shakes.

See how each one isn't trying to say everything? It's clear. Focused. Grounded in lived experience.

Think of everyone in the same arena as a book. You're writing *a chapter* in it. Or maybe only a page. This is your *niche*.

For example:

- If your *niche* is success, are you helping people **define** it on their own terms?
- Are you helping them **balance** success with well-being?
- Are you teaching people to stop chasing and **start being** successful?

All three are powerful, but they're not the same.

Think about what is missing in your arena that you wish someone had told you sooner. What was the gap in the conversation that **you** noticed? What frustrated you, confused you, or kept you stuck?

3. What's the Theme?
Sometimes your message is hidden inside your hardest moments. The breakdowns. The betrayals. The silence.
That's where truth lives. That's where your *true voice* is forged.

What pattern has followed you through different seasons?

- Have you always found yourself in rooms where your voice felt silenced, and now you help others speak up?
- Did you spend years trying to fit in, and now you teach people to belong to themselves?
- Were you always the helper, fixer, or the one who held things together until you burned out and had to learn how to heal?

4. Don't Be Afraid of Simplicity
Most people overlook their *true voice* because it feels **too simple**. But that's the point. You've lived with it so long, it feels obvious. But to someone else, it's life-changing.

What's obvious to you is a revelation to someone else.

Let it be simple. Let it be clear. Let it sound like something you wish you had told your younger self early on.

My True Voice

When I look back, I see how much of my life was shaped by silence. Shrinking. Shapeshifting. Trying to be what others needed me to be. It wasn't until I found my own voice—raw, imperfect, and honest—that things began to shift.

That's why I teach it now.
The day I found my *true voice*, everything changed.
It liberated **me**.
When I speak about **true voice**, I'm speaking from the very thing that saved me.

It gave me belonging.
It gave me access.
I could walk into any room, any space, and know I **have** authority.
Because I carry ancient knowledge, and the soul *remembers*.

Yes, I teach power. Yes, I speak about authority.
But the lifeblood of everything I do is this:

Your *true voice* **is** your **power.**

◇◇◇◇◇

Chapter Summary

Your voice is the sacred message your life has been trying to speak all along. And when you finally bring that truth to light—filtered through your personality, shaped by your story, and expressed in your own language—you make an impact. You become recognisable to the very souls your voice was meant to reach. When your voice is clear, your people will find you, and the world will feel your presence.

◇◇◇

Soul Reflection Questions

1. What core truth has life taught you over and over again, no matter how much you tried to avoid it?

2. What conversations do you keep finding yourself in—ones that make you feel alive, grounded, or lit up?

3. What moment in your life shaped the way you now see the world?

4. What part of your story have you been afraid to share, but know carries power for someone else?

5. What message would you share with the world even if no one applauded?

6. What specific frustration, pain, or gap in your industry or space do you feel uniquely called to speak into?

7. What does your younger self most need to hear from you right now?

8. When people listen to you, what do they often say they feel or recall about you?

9. If your story could speak, what would be its central message?

10. What message do you carry that feels like home to your soul, and how might that message serve someone who feels lost?

CHAPTER THIRTEEN

THE POWER OF YOUR HUMAN DESIGN

The Myth of Originality

Let's address the fear many of us secretly carry: that someone is already doing what we want to do. They probably are. And that's okay.

Let's say you and someone else both teach about healing after heartbreak. One of you might approach it through neuroscience. The other, through poetry. One of you brings softness. The other brings fire. Same message. Different *design*.

And people will resonate with **you** because of the way your soul delivers healing.

What Is Design, Really?

When I say *design*, I'm talking about the **architecture** of your soul. The way you naturally express truth, move through the world, and *channel* your purpose. This includes:

- **Your energy.** Are you magnetic, calm, fiery, grounded?
- **Your personality.** Quirky? Intense? Funny? Calm?
- **Your creative expression.** Do you express best through writing, images, voice, or movement?
- **Your passions.** What do you **love** to do so much it feels like play?
- **Your modality.** Do you coach, speak, write, paint, dance, film, or perform?
- **Your Human Design energy type.** That beautiful blueprint of how you connect to others.

No two *designs* are the same. Even if you have some of the same elements as someone else, your expression of that type will still be uniquely **yours.**

The Power of Human Design

If you haven't explored it yet, Human Design is an energetic system developed by Alan Robert Krabower. It maps how you were uniquely built to operate, decide, and impact the world. It's a fusion of astrology, the I Ching, Kabbalah, and the chakra system, and it offers incredibly specific insight. Think of it as your soul's instruction manual:

- How you make aligned decisions.
- How your energy is meant to flow.
- How you best express your truth.
- What kind of environments and people nourish you.
- What shadows and gifts you carry in your chart.

Your Human Design shows **how** you express who you are. For example:

- **Manifesting Generators** move fast, follow joy, and switch lanes when needed.

- **Projectors** guide others rather than do the grind themselves, and are most powerful when invited in.

- **Reflectors** are here to mirror the truth of their environment, and thrive in the right community.

- **Manifestors** initiate new movements and need freedom to act on inner urges.

- **Generators** are built for mastery, joy, and deeply satisfying work.

When you understand your *design*, things start to click. You stop pushing yourself to be like everyone else. You stop apologising for what makes you different. You stop muting the parts of you that make you magnetic.

You finally **feel at home.**

Examples of Design in Action

Let's look at a few examples:

1. The Storyteller Coach.

Many people help others rediscover their confidence. You do it through **storytelling.** You share personal narratives, metaphors, raw journal entries, and your clients **feel** it. You **touch people.**

2. The Soft-Spoken Speaker.

Someone else in your field is bold, charismatic, and fills a room. But you? You're soft. Gentle. You pause between words. And people **lean in.** You don't energise a crowd, you **anchor** them. You don't need to be loud to be powerful. You just need to be **truthful.**

3. The Artist of Healing.

Some might teach trauma healing through coaching. You teach it through **dance.** Or **film.** Or **visual arts.** And for the people who speak your language, your work becomes a **lifeline.**

Your *design* chooses **how** your *channel* flows. Trust it.

Why This Matters to Your Purpose

Your *design* is the frequency that makes your true voice unforgettable. Your realness. Your rhythm. Your vibe. Here's how you begin to embrace the power of your design:

Observe Yourself in Flow. What are you doing when you feel most alive? Teaching? Creating? Moving? Being still? Pay attention. That's your natural delivery system.

Accept the Quirks. Maybe you cry when you speak. Maybe you use your hands a lot. Maybe you can't work within a rigid structure. That's not a flaw, that's your flavour. Own it.

Use Your Human Design as a Tool (Not a Rule). Let it guide you, not box you in. If it resonates, explore how it aligns with your lived experience. Use it to affirm what you already **feel** to be true.

Refuse to Filter Yourself. Don't edit your essence. Don't water down your story. Don't trade your originality for acceptance. You were sent to **wake people up.**

Your Design Is Not Random, It's Sacred

The way you were designed—the **passions** you carry, the curiosity that tugs at your spirit, the *gifts* that feel second nature—none of it is accidental. Every piece of you was intentionally woven together to serve your purpose on this earth.

But purpose requires wholeness. It calls you to bring all of your mind, your heart, your creativity, your pain, and your joy into alignment with the assignment within you.

It can be hard to understand how the different parts of us fit into a singular purpose. We try to compartmentalise, to choose one *gift* and discard another. But the soul is not linear. It is layered. And if we stay curious long enough, if we keep exploring the whispers within us instead of silencing them, each gift will eventually find its rightful place. The puzzle will start to assemble itself through grace.

Storytelling: More Than a Medium

I once believed my **passion** for storytelling was about writing scripts, directing films, or publishing books. And on the surface, it was. But over time, I came to understand that my soul didn't come here just to write stories. It also came to **read** them within other people. I began to see that my love for story was a divine key. It wasn't the destination, it was the doorway. The more I studied narrative, the more I understood humanity.

Now, when someone speaks about their life—their heartbreaks, their detours, their doubts—I see a tapestry. I see a soul mid-*transformation*. They might see obstacles, delays, or confusion, but I see rhythm, purpose, and initiation. I see a soul being shaped by the very fire they're trying to escape.

This is where coaching has become more than a career. It's a sacred assignment. I hold space for others not just to speak, but to see the divine in their own unfolding. I mirror back the truth that their life is not a series of random events, but a soul-scripted journey.

In that space, healing happens. I help them *remember* who they are, why they came, and why their path, no matter how chaotic or confusing, has always been leading them home.

Cherish the Mystery

So I say to you: love your *design*. Even the parts you don't yet understand. Even the **passions** that don't seem to fit. They are all part of your soul's architecture.

The soul is never in a rush, but it is always precise. In time, the dots will connect. And you will look back and realised it was all sacred. All needed. All divine.

Keep walking. Keep wondering. Your purpose is not something you must strive for, it's something you're already moving towards.

The more you understand and embrace how you're built, the more powerful your presence becomes. You will never be everyone's cup of tea. But for the people you were built to serve, you'll be the missing piece they didn't even know they were searching for.

Let your *design* guide the delivery of your *true voice*. Let it amplify your uniqueness.

Remind the world that nobody does it like you do.

◇◇◇◇◇

Chapter Summary

You were divinely designed to deliver your message in a way only **you** can. Your *design* is the frequency of your magic. Whether it's through softness or fire, structure or flow, your *design* is the way your soul delivers healing. Trust it. Own it. Because when you express your truth through your *design*, you stop trying to be seen and start being *remembered*.

◇◇◇

Soul Reflection Questions

1. When do I feel the most **myself**? Alive, unfiltered, and magnetic?

2. What's my natural way of expressing truth—through words, movement, visuals, stillness, or something else?

3. What kind of healing or *transformation* do people often experience just by being in my presence?

4. In what ways has life already been showing me how I'm meant to deliver my message?

5. Have I ever diluted or hidden parts of my design to fit in or be accepted?

6. What quirks in my expression actually make me powerful?

7. How does my energy shift when I operate from my design versus when I try to be someone else?

8. If I trusted that my design was divine, how would I show up differently in the world?

9. What is one part of my essence I've been holding back that I'm ready to own fully?

10. If my life were the delivery system of my purpose, what would I say **through** it without words?

CHAPTER FOURTEEN

THE POWER OF YOUR IDENTITY

There comes a moment in every journey when we must look at the path that shaped us. **Who we've been, who we are, and who we're becoming** before we can fully reclaim our **identity**. You can't show up powerfully in the world if you're still hiding from your story. You can't lead from wholeness if you're still at war with your roots.

The world will try to convince you that your identity is a liability. That it makes you **too much** or **not enough**. But I'm here to remind you that your identity is your superpower. It's what **equips** you.

The Parts You've Been Told to Hide

Maybe you've been taught to tone down your accent. To minimise your culture. To avoid sharing **too much** of your story. To dress differently. Speak differently. **Be** different. Because somewhere along the way, the world said you would **be more accepted if you're less you.**

So you learned how to shrink. How to perform. How to present a polished, palatable version of yourself that wouldn't ruffle feathers. But what did it cost you?

Connection.
Confidence.
Clarity.

You can't connect with the people you're here to serve if you're pretending to be someone else. The people you're meant to lead are looking for **you**, not your mask.

The Gift in Your Background

Where you came from provided the soil where your roots grew deep. It's the climate where your voice was shaped. It's the landscape where your fire was ignited.

Your culture, your upbringing, your family dynamics, your traumas and triumphs—all of it contributes to your **angle**. And that **angle** is what gives your purpose its **unique edge**.

How to Reclaim Your Identity

Reclaiming your identity isn't just about looking back. It's about integrating what you find there. Here are some guiding questions to help you reconnect with the power in your identity:

1. What makes me feel most at home in myself?
It might be the food you eat. The music you play. The languages you speak. The traditions you still hold onto. These are your **anchors**.

2. Where have I felt I had to trade authenticity for acceptance?
Call it out. Then call **yourself** back. You're no longer required to shrink to belong.

3. What parts of my story have I been hiding or avoiding?
That pain or shame you avoid might be the very place your message is buried. Go there with compassion. There's gold hidden in the shadows.

4. What values were handed to me, and which ones do I choose for myself?

This is where healing happens. You get to decide what stays and what ends with you.

5. How has my background uniquely equipped me for the message I now carry?

Maybe your upbringing taught you resilience. Maybe your culture gave you rhythm. Maybe your survival gave you depth. All of it has built the foundation for your now.

Nothing is wasted.

A Refugee Turns Speaker

He was once told that his story was too heavy for mainstream audiences. That no one would connect with his past. Today, it's the reason people fly him across the world to speak.

His full story doesn't weaken his authority; it is his **authority**.

A Stay-at-Home Mother Becomes a Coach

She thought her identity as a mother would disqualify her from being seen as a leader. But when she began to lead from that space—when she spoke to burnout, to invisibility, to devotion—she built a tribe.

Her identity **wasn't** an obstacle to living her purpose. It was her *portal* to it.

An Afro-diasporic Creative Builds Her Empire

She grew up in a world that didn't reflect her beauty or her story. For years, she tried to fit into moulds that weren't made for her. But when she started creating from her **culture**—her language, her food, her rhythm, her art—her work began to **resonate**. Not just in her community, but globally.

People are hungry for **truths**. Sharing your identity can *channel* your *true voice*.

Identity is Who You *Choose* to Be

Your identity is a living, breathing story, and you get to **rewrite the narrative.**
You get to reframe what was painful.
You get to reclaim what was lost.
You get to revive what still matters.

You get to carry your ancestors' wisdom while breaking their chains. Honour your culture while expanding its possibilities, hold the past with tenderness, and shape the future with boldness.

◇◇◇◇◇

Chapter Summary

Your identity is the sacred soil from which your purpose grows. When you stop hiding who you are and start honouring where you come from, your story becomes a beacon. So, bring all of you—your accent, your background, your rhythm, your truth—because the world needs the real you, unfiltered and purposeful.

◇◇◇

Soul Reflection Questions

1. What parts of my identity have I been taught to tone down or hide, and why?

2. In what ways have I tried to perform or present a version of myself to fit in?

3. What elements of my story feel too disparate or uncomfortable, and how can I begin to reclaim them as sacred?

4. What cultural practices, traditions, or memories make me feel most at home in myself?

5. How has my background uniquely shaped the message I'm here to share?

6. What values from my upbringing do I want to keep, and which ones am I ready to release?

7. What wounds or challenges from my past might carry the wisdom I'm meant to teach?

8. Who do I become when I stop apologising for my story?

9. What would it look like to lead from my **true** identity instead of a polished persona?

10. If I fully embraced my identity as sacred, how would I show up to fulfil my purpose?

CHAPTER FIFTEEN

THE POWER OF YOUR BRAND

If you've done the inner work to discover your unique voice, design, and identity, then it's time to bring all of your parts together into something the world can recognise and respond to: your brand.

A brand is not just colours, logos, or fonts. It's not just a website or a slogan. Those are the way it is expressed. **Your brand is the feeling people get when they encounter you.**

It's the echo you leave in a room after you've spoken. It's what people whisper about you when you're not there, and what they think of when they need exactly what you offer.

Maybe your difference is the warmth in your voice. Maybe it's your fiery energy, or the softness that disarms people. Maybe it's the way you bring humour into heavy things, or how you simplify what others complicate.

Whatever it is, you need to bring it into the light.

Your Brand Is the Representation of Your Difference

A magnetic brand has three things:

- Authenticity. A brand is not about trying to impress. It's about being fully expressed. When your *true voice* is grounded in who you are, your brand becomes magnetic because people can tell it's real.

- Clarity. People follow certainty. You know exactly what you stand for, who you serve, and what problem you solve. If someone lands on your website or social media page and watches a video or hears you speak, your brand speaks to who you intend to serve.

- Consistency. The world needs to see you show up again and again with the same energy, the same truth, the same message. You become known by being clear over time. That's how trust is built—and trust is the currency of a powerful brand.

Build a Brand That *Feels* Like You

Let's imagine your purpose is to help people heal through storytelling. Your *design* might be emotional, soft, poetic. Your identity might come from growing up in a culture that silenced emotions. Your *true voice* might be focused on inner child work.

So your brand might look like:

- A podcast with soul-stirring storytelling.
- Visuals with warm earth tones and nostalgic music.
- Copy that feels like a journal entry.
- Offers that invite people to feel, cry, release, and *transform*.

Here are questions to help you shape a brand that reflects your truth and reveals what's within:

- What emotions do I want people to feel when they encounter me?
- What colours, textures, or sounds reflect my energy?
- What's the *transformation* I offer, and how does that show up in my content?
- How can I show up in a way that feels easy, aligned, and sustainable?
- What are three words people often use to describe me? Are they reflected in my brand?

Chapter Summary

Your brand is the reflection of your soul, your story, your presence, and your purpose made visible. When you show up in your truth, with clarity, consistency, and authenticity, your brand stops being a strategy and starts being a **legacy**. The world needs **you**, fully realised, fully feeling, and fully expressed.

◇◇◇

Soul Reflection Questions

1. What feeling do I want people to walk away with after encountering me or my work?

2. What makes my presence memorable, and how can I bring more of that into my brand?

3. Where am I still trying to fit into someone else's mould instead of honouring my own essence?

4. What are three truths I stand for, and how can I express them clearly through my content?

5. In what ways can I create a brand that feels like home to both me and my audience?

6. What parts of my personality, story, or energy have I been hiding that actually make me magnetic?

7. What *transformation* do I offer, and how is that reflected in the way I show up online or in person?

8. How can I consistently share my voice without burning out or compromising my authenticity?

9. What does a brand built around my *true voice* **look** and **feel** like?

10. If my brand was a living expression of my soul's message, what would it sound like, look like, and move like?

CHAPTER SIXTEEN

THE POWER OF YOUR MESSAGE

You know what you carry. You know how you're designed. You know the presence you bring. But can you say it in a sentence? Can you communicate your soul's work **so clearly** that someone who hears it immediately knows you're the one they've been looking for?

Your Message is the Bridge Between Your Purpose and the People who Need It

A strong message doesn't try to say everything. It says the right thing, to the right person, at the right moment. It's the beating heart of **why** you do what you do and **who** it's for.

- What *transformation* do you offer?
- Why should someone care about what you do?
- What makes your voice the one they need to hear right now?

Here's how you can begin crafting or refining yours:

1. The Person You're Speaking To.

Your message should feel like a mirror. If a reader can't see themselves in it, they'll scroll past it. Think:

- **Who are they?**
- **What season of life are they in?**
- **What are they silently struggling with?**

2. The Problem You Solve.

This is the arena you're in and the **specific pain** your audience feels.

Let these inspire you:

- 'I help purpose-driven leaders find the clarity and courage to speak with power.'
- 'I teach creatives how to turn their personal stories into profitable brands.'
- 'I help burned-out professionals rediscover their joy and redesign a life that fits.'
- 'I support immigrant women to embrace their roots and rise with confidence.'

3. The Promise You're Making.

What happens when they follow you, work with you, or listen to you? What changes?

Where Your Message Lives

Once you have it, your message becomes the compass for everything:

- Your website headline.
- Your social media bio.
- The theme of your content.
- The energy behind your offers.
- The words you say when someone asks you **what you do.**

When your message is clear, everything else aligns.

Just like you, your message will evolve. It might get deeper. Sharper. Simpler. So don't wait until you think it's perfect. Start with where you are. Speak what you know. Share what you've lived.

Let your message **mature with you.** That's **growth.**

Soul Reflective Questions

1. Who do I feel most drawn to help, and what is their silent struggle?

2. What problem do I feel deeply called to solve, and why does it matter to me?

3. If I had to describe the transformation I offer in one sentence, what would it be?

4. Is the message I'm currently sharing true to the version of me I've become?

5. How can I make my message clearer, bolder, or more rooted in real transformation?

THE RISE

The final phase. A return to self—elevated. You now lead with wisdom, speak with soul, and move with alignment. This is your era of soulful power and visibility.

Chapters

CHAPTER SEVENTEEN

THE CIRCLE OF MIRRORS

By now, you have realised that you have no competition.

You have uncovered what makes you unique, and you stand in the confidence that you are one of a kind. There is no duplicate of you. Your journey has been deeply personal, but it was never meant to be walked alone.

Now, it is time to find and build your *soul community*; a circle of people who, like you, are walking their own path of *transformation*. These are the ones who will hold a mirror to your soul, reflecting your growth, your struggles, and your potential back to you.

But before you step into this sacred circle, you must understand something crucial: **everyone in your community is in their own battle.**

The People on the Same Path

You are gathering like-minded, **like-souled individuals.** People who have answered their call to break free, who are facing their own inner battles, and who, like you, are working to rewrite their destiny.

This means that:

- They are also healing.
- They are also unlearning.
- They are also confronting the whispers of doubt, fear, and old beliefs that try to pull them back.

And because of this, they will not always get it right. Neither will you.

There will be moments of insecurity. Moments of comparison. Moments when the shadows of your old beliefs show up in new ways—perhaps as jealousy, self-doubt, or the fear of being outshined.

This is the real test of a soul community. Can you see beyond these moments? Can you hold space for each other's growth without judgment? Can you rise together?

The Purpose of Soul Community

Soul work is sacred, but it is also *hard*. You need people who will:

- **Remind** you who you are when you forget.
- **Call you out** when you start slipping back into old beliefs.
- **See your greatness** when you are too blinded by fear to recognise it yourself.
- **Support** you in moments of self-doubt without trying to fix you.
- **Challenge** you when you start playing small.

Without a *soul community*, the journey is lonelier, heavier, and more dangerous. With them, you become stronger, braver, and more committed to your purpose.

How to Build and Nurture Your Soul Community

- **Be Authentic.** Your people can only find you if you show up as your true self. You cannot attract aligned souls while pretending to be something you're not.
- **Give What You Seek.** If you want support, offer support. If you want encouragement, be encouraging. Soul communities thrive on reciprocity.
- **Call Each Other Higher.** Growth is not always comfortable. Be the kind of person who challenges your community to be their best self, with love and truth.
- **Celebrate Each Other.** Their success does not take away from yours. Learn to see their wins as evidence that you, too, can rise.
- **Release the Fear of Outgrowing Others.** Some people will not evolve with you, and that's okay. Let them go with love.

The New Battle

Even in a soul-aligned community, your *old demons* will find new ways to creep in.

- **Comparison.** Feeling like you are not good enough because someone else is shining.
- **Jealousy.** Wishing you had what another person has, instead of using it as inspiration.
- **Imposter Syndrome.** Doubting your place in the circle, wondering if you truly belong.
- **Fear of Rejection.** Holding back your full self because you fear you won't be accepted.

When these feelings arise, do not run from them. *Examine them:*

- Where does this fear come from?
- What is this feeling trying to teach me?
- How can I turn this into an opportunity for growth?

Because the truth is that if you cannot celebrate others, you are not yet free.

Your *soul community* is not a place for competition. It is a place for *collective rising*. The success, power, and *transformation* you see in them is a reflection of what is also possible for you.

Now, as you step deeper into this circle, you must make a choice: will you let old fears separate you, or will you **rise together?**

◇◇◇◇◇

Chapter Summary

This chapter explores the power of soul-aligned community—
people who reflect your truth, challenge your growth, and
walk alongside you in *transformation*. While your journey is
personal, it's not meant to be isolated. True *soul communities*
are about rising together through authenticity, mutual support,
and love. Along the way, old patterns like comparison, jealousy,
or imposter syndrome may resurface, but these are not signs to
retreat. They are mirrors asking you to heal deeper. In a soul
community, your greatness is reflected back to you, and together
you become part of a **collective rising**.

◇◇◇

Soul Reflection Questions

1. How can I show up more authentically in my
   relationships?

2. Where do I still feel triggered by others' success or
   presence?

3. Who in my life reflects my soul's truth and calls me
   higher?

4. What part of me still fears being fully seen, supported,
   or celebrated?

5. What kind of soul community do I desire, and am I
   being that for others?

CHAPTER EIGHTEEN

THE NEXT MOUNTAIN

You have fought. You have grown. You have stepped into your power. You have shattered the limits that once held you back. You have become the version of yourself that, not too long ago, you could only dream of being. And yet, **you are not done.**

The soul does not crave comfort. It does not desire stillness. It does not celebrate an endpoint. The moment you stop reaching, stop expanding, stop setting your sights higher, is the moment your soul begins to wither. This is why you felt suffocated in the beginning: you were not growing. Your soul knew you were capable of **more**, and it refused to settle.

The Illusion of Arrival

You have broken past what you once thought impossible. You have stepped into the unknown and made it your home. You have rewritten the story you were given and reclaimed the pen. But here's the challenge: if you don't set a new vision to chase something bigger, you will start to feel stuck again.

Purpose is an evolving force. It is a moving target. You were never meant to stop.

Many people fall into the trap of believing that once they reach a certain level of success, they are done. They assume that once they heal, build their business, write their book, or finally find their purpose, the journey is over. But this is an **illusion**.

The moment you stop climbing, you begin to decay.

After I had published two books, made two films, and completed my coaching certification, I felt like I had achieved everything I had once dreamed of achieving. I had done it. I had reached the mountaintop. And yet, to my surprise, I began to feel restless. An unshakable sadness crept in. I was lost, even though I had accomplished everything I set out to do.

I poured these feelings out to my mentor, a man who had known me for over ten years. 'What you need is another goal,' he chuckled.

He was right. As soon as I applied to return to university to pursue my Honours and Ph.D., my soul rose again. **Up on your feet now,** it said. **We've got work to do.**

You are in charge, now. You know how the game works. Don't wait for someone to come and remind you of what your next level is. You're your own boss: act like one.

Growth is infinite. There is always another layer, another level, another mountain to climb. This is why so many people experience post-success depression. After they win the award, after they reach the goal, after they achieve what they thought was the pinnacle, they find themselves feeling lost. This is because they have misunderstood the nature of purpose.

You are meant to *keep climbing.* This is the cycle:

1. You set a goal that feels impossible.
2. You push past your limits to reach it.
3. You achieve it and feel victorious.

4. Discomfort creeps in, and the whispers return.

5. It's time for **more**.

Why Your Soul Craves More

You were never meant to stop at **good enough**. You were never meant to hit a ceiling and call it a day. Your soul does not stop evolving just because you've achieved something great.

You were designed for *expansion, evolution, and continuous becoming*. This is why the most fulfilled people in the world never stop reaching. They understand something that most people don't: *growth is a lifelong journey*.

- The best athletes don't win one championship and retire. They go for more.

- The greatest artists don't create one masterpiece and quit. They keep creating.

- The most powerful leaders don't solve one problem and walk away. They take on bigger ones.

But here's where most people hesitate. After all the battles they've fought, after all the demons they've faced, *they fear setting the bar higher*.

They wonder:

- What if I fail at this next thing?
- What if I lose everything I've built?
- What if I'm not as good as I think I am?

This fear is normal. You have been here before. In the beginning, you doubted yourself. You weren't sure you could break free. But you did.

It's time to do it again.

How to Find Your Next Mountain

If you are feeling lost, restless, or stagnant, it is a sign that your soul is ready for a new challenge. It is not an indication that you are ungrateful or incapable, it is a *calling* for expansion.

Here's how to navigate this stage:

1. Recognise That Growth is a Lifelong Journey.
The idea that you will no longer need to grow is false. The best leaders, the most fulfilled people, and those who leave the greatest impact are those who never stop learning. You must train yourself to fall in love with evolution, to crave new challenges rather than fear them.

2. Acknowledge the Signs of Restlessness.
When your soul is ready for a new mountain, it will send signals. You may feel:

- Unmotivated, even after achieving success.
- A deep inner restlessness.
- A feeling of stagnation.
- A loss of excitement for things you once loved.

These are signs that it's time to **grow** again.

3. Ask Yourself: What is the Next Evolution of My Purpose?
Purpose is fluid. It evolves as you evolve. So, what is your soul asking for now? Do you need to step into leadership? Share your story on a bigger stage? Mentor others? Write the book? Enter a new field? The key is to listen to what is calling you next.

4. Don't Be Afraid to Start Again.
Starting again does not mean you are back at zero. It means you are leveling up. Every time you take on a new challenge, you bring with you all the wisdom, experience, and strength from your past battles. You are e *evolving into* **mastery**.

5. Set a New Vision and Commit to It.

If you don't define your next goal, life will feel meaningless. Set a bold, exciting vision—something that stretches you, scares you, and forces you to grow. And then, go after it with everything you have.

Your Growth Template

1. **Set the Next Impossible Goal.** What is something that scares you? Something so big it feels insane? Set it. Write it down. Declare it. If it doesn't scare you, it's too small.

2. **Break It Down.** You climb a mountain step by step. What are the small actions that will get you there?

3. **Master Discomfort.** Every time you stretch, it will feel uncomfortable. Get used to it. Learn to love it. Let it be a sign that you're on the right path.

4. **Surround Yourself with Bigger Thinkers.** The people around you should challenge you. If you are the biggest dreamer in your circle, you are in the wrong circle.

5. **Celebrate, Then Set the Bar Higher.** Once you achieve something, take a moment to acknowledge it. But don't stay there too long. Set the next goal before the old excitement fades.

6. **Stay Curious.** Read, explore, ask questions. The more you learn, the more you grow. The more you grow, the more you see what is possible.

7. **Be Relentless.** Growth is not for the faint of heart. It requires resilience. It demands that you keep going, no matter what.

So, what is the next impossible thing you will set your sights on?

◇◇◇◇◇

Chapter Summary

Once you have achieved significant milestones and overcome personal barriers, the challenge is to set new, even bigger goals. Purpose is an evolving force. The soul craves expansion, and restlessness after reaching a goal is a sign that you are ready for the next challenge. Embrace discomfort and consistently seek new heights. It urges you to never settle, always raise the bar, and see failure as a necessary step on the path to a new level of achievement.

◇◇◇

Soul Reflection Questions

1. How can you ensure that you continue to grow, even after achieving your current goals?

2. What is the next big, scary goal that excites you, even though it feels impossible?

3. What limiting beliefs are trying to hold you back from setting that goal?

4. How can you learn to embrace discomfort as a sign of growth, and how will you use it to propel yourself forward?

5. Who do you need to surround yourself with to keep challenging and stretching your potential?

CHAPTER NINETEEN

THE POWER OF BALANCE

Rising requires rhythm. It's about how high you go and how grounded you stay while you go there. It's about building and sustaining. *Balance* is about the sacred rhythm that allows you to move with grace, lead with strength, and live with peace.

Why *Balance* Matters on the Journey

When you start stepping into purpose, it can feel like everything depends on you. You want to show up. You want to give it your all. You want to be consistent, visible, valuable.

But what happens when your cup runs dry?

Too many powerful voices burn out because they've mistaken busyness for purpose. They hustle without harmony. They serve others and forget themselves. They mistake urgency for importance.

Balance isn't optional if you want to go the distance. It'ss the backbone of sustainability, and the quiet discipline that **keeps your light burning without burning out.**

The Rhythm of Rise

You weren't designed to be **on** all the time. You were made for cycle: action and rest, speaking and listening, building and being. Even nature honours rhythm.

There's sunrise and sunset.
There's inhale and exhale.
There's summer and winter.
There's creation and restoration.

Rhythm is wisdom. It reminds you that pausing is about **power**.

Boundaries: The Gatekeepers of Your Energy

Balance is also about what you no longer tolerate.

Your **boundaries** are the gates that protect your vision, your wellness, your peace. You can't create powerful work if your energy is constantly leaking. When you don't set **boundaries**:

- Resentment grows.
- Your creativity gets cluttered.
- Your intuition becomes faint.
- Your message becomes diluted.
- Not every opportunity is for you.
- Not everyone should have access to you.
- Saying yes to everyone else often means saying no to yourself.

You have **the right and the responsibility** to decide how your time, energy, and presence are spent.

Here are a few signs that you may need to restore *balance*:

- You feel overwhelmed even by small tasks.
- You're constantly tired but can't rest.
- You're giving your best energy to things that don't fulfill you.
- You're struggling to hear your own intuition.
- You've started resenting your own *mission*.

If this is you, **pause**. Return to your sacred rituals. Recommit to rhythm and *balance*.

Sacred Self-Care is a Leadership Tool

Self-care is the space where you check in with your soul, the rituals that keep you grounded, and the commitment to your emotional, mental, spiritual, and physical well-being. It's strategic. It's how you show up with enough to share.

Some of your most profound clarity, insight, and creative breakthroughs will come in the spaces you allow yourself to rest. When you take care of yourself, everyone you serve benefits.

Balance Is a Practice

Listen daily. Practice self-awareness. Adjust as you go. Stay attuned to the shifts in your season. You'll fall out of *balance* sometimes. That's okay. What matters is that you notice it, and you return. Move in rhythm, guard your energy, and honour your rest to **evolve**.

◇◇◇◇◇

Chapter Summary

Rising to your full potential is about maintaining rhythm and *balance*. The key to long-term success lies in mastering the rhythm of life—knowing when to take action and when to rest. **Boundaries** protect your energy, which is just as essential as practicing sacred self-care and rest. True *balance* is about constant realignment to ensure you're nourishing yourself while pursuing your purpose.

◇◇◇

Soul Reflective Questions

1. How do I currently maintain *balance* between my work and personal life?

2. What *boundaries* do I need to set to protect my energy and focus on what truly matters?

3. What sacred self-care practices can I incorporate into my routine to stay grounded and aligned?

4. What rhythm do I need to cultivate in my life to sustain my rise and prevent burnout?

5. How do I respond when I feel out of *balance*, and how can I better recognise the signs earlier?

CHAPTER TWENTY

THE SOUL'S
TRUE PATH

You have stepped onto the path that was always meant for you.

This is a journey of reconciliation. You have aligned yourself with something far greater than personal ambition: a collaboration with spirit itself.

From this point on, you are no longer walking alone.

The Shift: From Flesh to Soul

Something is changing. You feel it. It is subtle at first, like a whisper in the wind, a deeper knowing in your gut. But as you continue on this path, the whispers grow louder, and you begin to realise that you are not the same.

Your old self sought answers from external sources: teachers, systems, traditions. But now, the guidance is coming from within. The voice of your soul is getting clearer, and it is being supported by something even greater: the presence of ancestors, the energy of the unseen, the universal intelligence that has been waiting for you to step into your *calling*. The once who knew your name long before you were born.

Your decisions, your actions, and your perception of life are all shifting because you are moving with deep spiritual alignment.

This is the awakening of the *true voice*.

At the time I discovered my own *true voice*, I didn't know I was changing. I thought I was just tired of pretending and performing; playing roles that looked right but didn't feel authentic. I was still operating from what I had been taught: survive, succeed, stay safe. But as I kept moving through life, especially after confronting my past and reclaiming parts of my story, I started noticing something different within me.

It was subtle at first. But then one day, I went for a walk. The sun was just beginning to set, the park around me hushed except for the birds. I recall how still everything felt, how clear the air seemed. And then, out of nowhere, a phrase resonated with my spirit: *true voice*.

I froze mid-step.

The words didn't come from my own scattered thoughts. They felt placed, precise. Like someone had been waiting to hand them to me at just the right moment. Before I could even fully grasp what they meant, the rest followed:

The world uses voice. What they need is true *voice.*

It hit me like a truth I had always known, but never articulated. The struggle, the disconnect, the constant striving people carry— it's not because they don't have a voice. It's because they aren't living from their true one. We've all been communicating from the moment we were born, through how we behave, how we dress, how we carry ourselves. But most of us are communicating through a mask, not our truth.

And that's why we suffer.

But I didn't run with it. Not at first.

The old me—the one still craving approval—brushed it off. I thought nobody would understand it. It was **too abstract, not polished enough, not ready.** I let those resonating words sit quietly inside me, thinking maybe they weren't for now.

Over time, the shift deepened. It wasn't just a phrase anymore, it became a way of living. My choices changed. My energy changed. I stopped wondering what people would think and started listening for the voice that had spoken to me that day in the park.

And that's when I understood: this wasn't about me finding a message. This was about the message finding me.

Even this book is not being written the way I once imagined. The old version of me would have waited for validation from a publisher, for someone to give me permission to speak. But my soul said **no. This isn't just your book. This is ours. This is sacred.** So I wrote. And I'm still writing. Because someone out there doesn't need perfection, they need **truth.** They need the sound of their own soul reflected back at them, so they can rise too.

You Are Now in Collaboration With Spirit

Spirit has always been with you. But now, you are aware of it. You are open to it. You will begin to notice synchronicities— signs, symbols, repeated messages that seem too precise to be coincidence. You will receive intuitive nudges that feel like deep, undeniable truths. Ideas will come to you out of nowhere, opportunities will align effortlessly, and your path will unfold in ways you could never have planned yourself. This is the language of spirit.

You have entered into *divine collaboration.* Cultivate an openness to it. You must learn to trust the unseen and strengthen your connection to the spiritual realm.

- **Silence the Noise.** The voice of spirit is subtle, quiet, and easily drowned out by external distractions. Create intentional space for silence in your life. Meditate, take walks without music, sit in stillness. The more silence you allow, the clearer the whispers become.

- **Trust the Nudges.** The universe speaks through subtle nudges, gut feelings, and unexplainable knowing. When something keeps coming back to you—an idea, a dream, a call to action—trust it. Lean in. Take the step.

- **Engage in Spiritual Practices.** Develop rituals that strengthen your spiritual connection. This can be through prayer, meditation, journaling, energy work, or anything that helps you feel aligned with the unseen.

- **Seek Symbols & Signs.** Spirit often communicates through repeated patterns: angel numbers, animals, dreams, unexpected messages from people. Pay attention. Keep a journal of these moments and reflect on their meaning.

- **Embody the Abundance Mindset.** If you are still thinking small, doubting your worth, or fearing failure, you are not fully trusting. Open yourself up to receive. Know that there is more than enough for you. Act from that place of abundance.

- **Listen to Your Soul's Voice.** The deeper you go, the clearer your inner voice becomes. You will start to recognise when something feels aligned and when it doesn't. This is soul guiding you. Honour it. Follow what feels expansive. Step away from what feels restrictive.

- **Surrender to the Path.** The path is unfolding. Your job is to walk it, to listen, and to trust that everything is happening in divine timing.✛

Opening Yourself to Receive

You have been conditioned to think that success is something you chase, something you force into existence. But you are now in a phase where your job is not to chase, it is to **allow**. The universe is ready to pour into you. The blessings, the opportunities, the guidance—it is already waiting. Open yourself to receive it.

- **Release Resistance.** Stop overthinking and doubting. Let go of the idea that you have to earn or prove your worth. You are already enough.

- **Be in a State of Gratitude.** Gratitude raises your frequency. The more you acknowledge the gifts already present in your life, the more you will attract.

- **Say Yes to Opportunities.** Spirit will send you openings. Doors will appear. Say yes, even if they scare you.

◇◇◇◇◇

Chapter Summary

This is a journey of spiritual alignment, where the guidance you seek comes from within, supported by the wisdom of spirit and the universe. As you move from survival to soul, you begin to recognise synchronicities and intuitive nudges that direct you toward your divine purpose. You are in collaboration with spirit. To deepen this connection, silence the noise, trust your inner nudges, and engage in spiritual practices. Success is about receiving by opening yourself to the guidance and abundance that the universe is ready to pour into you. Trust in the path and surrender to your journey.

◇◇◇

Soul Reflection Questions

1. What distractions in my life are drowning out the voice of my soul?

2. How do I currently receive messages from spirit, and how can I become more open to them?

3. In what ways have I noticed my intuition getting stronger?

4. Where am I still holding onto scarcity thinking, and how can I shift into an abundance mindset?

5. What is one small step I can take today to deepen my connection with spirit?

CHAPTER TWENTY-ONE

THE SHIFT
INTO DEPTH

You have crossed the bridge. You have stepped into your soul's path. You are moving differently. You are in alignment with your soul's purpose. Spirit is guiding you. This is just the beginning of a deeper, richer, and more expansive journey. Stay open. Stay receptive. Stay aligned.

Trust the path ahead.

The Shift: From Striving to Receiving

Up until now, much of your journey has been about breaking through resistance: external expectations, internal self-doubt, inherited beliefs. But once you fully align with your soul's purpose, the struggle begins to dissolve. The path doesn't necessarily get easier, but you stop fighting it. You start to flow with it instead.

This is because you are no longer acting alone. Whether you call it your higher self, divine guidance, ancestors, spirit guides, or simply intuition, you are now in conversation with something greater than yourself.

The Call to Go Deeper

Being on this path means that life as you once knew it will never be the same. The way you perceive the world, the way you make decisions, the way you operate changes.

You will begin to notice:

- A heightened sense of **intuition.** You will know things without knowing how you know them. Trust that.

- **Synchronicities** appearing everywhere. Conversations, signs, and unexpected opportunities will start aligning in ways that feel uncanny.

- A pull toward **stillness** and **introspection.** Silence will become more sacred. You will crave time alone to listen to what is being whispered to you.

- A **detachment** from old identities. You will feel yourself shedding roles, titles, and labels that no longer fit who you are *becoming.*

- A **new way of operating.** You no longer move through the world as just a body. You begin to operate as one with your soul.

This is the shift. And with it comes a new **responsibility:** to remain open, to receive, and to deepen the journey.

The Art of Receiving: Opening to Guidance

Receiving is an art. And yet, we have been taught to resist it.

For so long, we were conditioned to force our way forward. To push. To hustle. To prove our worth through effort. But when you step into alignment, that approach no longer works. This means deep listening. It means trusting the flow instead of fighting against it.

The journey requires you to *surrender.*

1. Recognise and Follow the Signs.

Spirit communicates through signs: patterns, synchronicities, and nudges that seem too perfect to be coincidence.

- Have you been seeing repeated numbers? 11:11, 222, 444?
- Have people been mentioning the same book, idea, or place to you over and over?
- Has an opportunity fallen into your lap that feels too aligned to ignore?

This is guidance for you. Follow where it leads.

2. Trust the Whispers.

Intuition is subtle. It will come as a whisper, a knowing, a feeling in your gut. The more you listen to it, the stronger it becomes.

Start honouring those small nudges, even if they don't make sense or challenge logic. Your soul knows things your mind does not.

3. Cultivate Stillness.

Your soul is always speaking. If you want to hear the voice of your soul, you have to create space for it to speak.

- **Spend time in silence daily.** Even five minutes of intentional stillness can shift everything.
- **Meditate.** Not to control the mind, but to witness it.
- **Walk in nature without distraction.** Listen to the wind. Feel the pulse of the earth beneath your feet.
- **Write.** Let your thoughts spill onto paper without judgment.

4. Deepen Your Connection with Spirit Guides

Once you step onto your soul's path, you are being supported, protected and guided. Your guides have always been here. They are simply waiting for you to open the door.

- **Speak to them.** Ask for their wisdom out loud, in prayer, or by journaling.
- **Use rituals.** Light a candle, sit in meditation, create a sacred space.
- **Pay attention to dreams.** Messages often come in symbols while you sleep.
- **Express gratitude.** The more you acknowledge their presence, the clearer their guidance will be.
- **Living as Soul: The Ultimate Shift**

You are a soul moving through the world. This shift will change everything. Your work. Your relationships. Your energy. The way you exist in the world. You are now force of nature in alignment with the divine.

- You will no longer make decisions out of fear. You will choose from trust.
- You will no longer crave external validation. You will move from inner knowing.
- You will no longer chase. You will attract.

And the deeper you go, the more the world will open up to you.

◇◇◇◇◇

Chapter Summary

You move through life in harmony with spirit, *transforming* from striving to receiving, and trusting in divine guidance and intuition. You will experience heightened awareness, synchronicities, and a deeper connection to silence. This chapter emphasises the importance of surrender: cultivating stillness, trusting intuitive whispers, and following signs that guide you. As you deepen your connection with spirit, the journey becomes one of co-creation with the universe: making choices from trust, inner knowing, and alignment with the divine which opens you to limitless possibilities.

◇◇◇

Soul Reflection Questions

1. How can I create more stillness to hear the voice of my soul?

2. What signs and synchronicities have been appearing in my life? What might they be guiding me toward?

3. How can I deepen my connection with my spirit guides and open myself up to their wisdom?

4. Where in my life am I still pushing instead of receiving?

5. Have I been ignoring any intuitive nudges? What would happen if I trusted them instead?

CHAPTER TWENTY-TWO

THE EVER-UNFOLDING JOURNEY

You have walked through fire. You have faced yourself, your fears, your doubts. You have reclaimed your voice, stepped into your power, and opened yourself to the deeper calling of your soul. As you stand at this new threshold, you understand that the journey is never over.

Every lesson, every experience, every moment of awakening has only been the foundation for what comes next: the unfolding, the deepening, the expansion.

Remain a Student of Life

The most powerful souls are not the ones who claim to have all the answers. They are the ones who remain curious, open, and humble in the face of life's infinite lessons. Even after all the wisdom you've gained, you will still be a student. And that is a *gift*.

- **Stay curious.** Never assume you know everything. Every day brings new insights.

- **Seek discomfort.** Growth happens at the edges of what feels safe.

- **Allow yourself to be guided.** Trust that your soul, your intuition, and your spirit guides are leading you where you need to go.

- **Release the need for certainty.** The more you surrender, the more magic unfolds.

Service: The Highest Expression of Purpose

When you first began this journey, it was about **you**: your **pain**, your *channel*, your *transformation*. But now, something has shifted.

True purpose is never just about the self. It is about **service.**

The wisdom you have gained is meant to be shared, to be given, to be used for something greater than yourself. Service can look like a simple conversation, an act of kindness, a willingness to be present for others in their own unfolding.

The more you give, the more you receive.

How to Integrate This Journey into Daily Life

It's easy to have deep realisations when reading a book like this, immersed in *transformation*. But how do you carry this forward in everyday life?

1. **Anchor into daily rituals.** Meditate, journal, move your body; do something each day that connects you to your soul.

2. **Listen to your intuition.** The answers are always within you, but you must create space to hear them.

3. **Stay flexible.** Your purpose may shift, evolve, take unexpected turns. Trust the process.

4. **Surround yourself with growth-minded people.** Your environment shapes your evolution. Find those who expand you.

5. **Celebrate every moment.** There is no rush. There is no end goal. There is only the unfolding.

A Final Reflection

Everything you have read, everything you have uncovered in yourself, is just the beginning. The soul's path is infinite, and you are now walking it with a new awareness, a new power, a new depth.

You are not the same person who started this book.

You have expanded.

You have awakened.

And you are still unfolding.

◇◇◇◇◇

Chapter Summary

Life is in constant motion, and so are you. The soul will always call for **more**. Remain a student of life, staying curious and allowing yourself to be guided. Purpose evolves from personal healing to **service**, and the wisdom you gain is meant to be shared. To integrate this journey into daily life, you must anchor yourself with daily rituals, trust your intuition, surround yourself with growth-minded people, stay flexible, and celebrate every moment. The journey is infinite, and with each step, you expand further into your true essence.

◇◇◇

Reflection Questions

1. In what ways can I begin to share the wisdom I've gained through my journey with others?

2. What discomfort in my life can I lean into for further personal growth?

3. How can I stay open to new growth and learning even when I feel I've reached a place of clarity?

4. How can I anchor spiritual practices into my daily routine to stay connected to my soul?

5. What can I celebrate about my journey so far, knowing that there is no end goal—just continuous unfolding?

A LETTER TO YOU

As you close this book, I want you to know this:

You were never lost.
You were never broken.
You were always meant to find your way back to yourself.

You are not alone.
You are not small.
You are not incapable.

You are a soul in motion, a voice that carries **power**, a force of light in this world.
There is no final destination, only the next step, and then the next.

Go forward. Speak your truth. Live your purpose. Trust your soul. The journey is yours now.

With love and infinite belief in you,

www.ingramcontent.com/pod-product-compliance
Lightning Source LLC
Chambersburg PA
CBHW031933090426
42811CB00002B/167